HARRAP'S

German

PHRASE BOOK

Compiled by
LEXUS
with
Horst Kopleck

HARRAP

London   Paris

First published in Great Britain 1989
by HARRAP BOOKS LTD
19-23 Ludgate Hill London EC4M 7PD

© *Harrap Books Ltd/Lexus Ltd* 1989

ISBN 0 245-54750-9

Printed in Great Britain by
Richard Clay Ltd,
Bungay, Suffolk

CONTENTS

INTRODUCTION

The phrase sections in this new book are concise and to the point. In each section you will find: a list of basic vocabulary; a selection of useful phrases; a list of common words and expressions that you will see on signs and notices. A full pronunciation guide is given for things you'll want to say or ask and typical replies to some of your questions are listed.

Of course, there are bound to be occasions when you want to know more. So this book allows for this by containing a two way German-English dictionary with a total of some 5,000 references. This will enable you to build up your German vocabulary, to make variations on the phrases in the phrase sections and to recognize more of the German words that you will see or hear when travelling about.

As well as this we have given a menu reader covering about 200 dishes and types of food — so that you will know what you are ordering! And, as a special feature, there is a section on colloquial German.

Speaking the language can make all the difference to your trip. So:

Viel Glück!
feel glewk
good luck!

and

Gute Reise!
gOOtuh rīzuh
have a good trip!

PRONUNCIATION

In the phrase sections of this book a pronunciation guide has been given by writing the German words as though they were English. So if you read out the pronunciation as English words a German person should be able to understand you. Some notes on this:

ew close to the sound as in 'few' or 'dew'
g as in 'get' or 'gone' (not as in 'gin')
i as in 'pie' or 'sky'
J as the 's' sound in 'leisure' or 'pleasure'
κ similar to the 'ch' sound in the way the Scots pronounce 'loch'
oo as in 'hook' or 'crook'
oo as in 'spoon' or 'moon'
ow as in 'how' or 'now'
uh like the 'e' in 'the' or in 'cover'

Letters in bold type in the pronunciation guide mean that this part of the word should be stressed.

hello
guten Tag; (*at night*) guten Abend
*gOOten tahk; gOOten **ahbent***

hi
hallo
hallo

good morning
guten Morgen
gOOten morgen

good afternoon
guten Tag
gOOten tahk

good evening
guten Abend
*gOOten **ahbent***

good night
gute Nacht
gOOtuh nahкt

pleased to meet you
freut mich
froyt mish

goodbye
auf Wiedersehen
owf veeder-zayn

cheerio
tschüs
tchewss

see you
bis dann
biss dan

GENERAL PHRASES

yes/no
ja/nein
ya/nīn

yes please
ja, bitte
ya bittuh

no thank you
nein, danke
nīn dankuh

please
bitte
bittuh

thank you/thanks
danke (schön)
dankuh (shurn)

thanks very much
vielen Dank
feelen dank

you're welcome
nichts zu danken
nishts tsoo danken

sorry
Entschuldigung
entshooldigoong

sorry? (*didn't understand*)
bitte?
bittuh

how are you?
wie geht's?
vee gayts

very well, thank you
danke, sehr gut
dankuh zair goot

and yourself?
und selbst?
oont zelpst

GENERAL PHRASES

excuse me (*to get attention*)
entschuldigen Sie bitte
entshooldigen zee bittuh

how much is it?
was kostet das?
vass kostet dass

can I . . .?
kann ich . . .?
kan ish

can I have . . .?
ich hätte gern . . .
ish hettuh gairn

I'd like to . . .
ich möchte gern . . .
ish murshtuh gairn

where is . . .?
wo ist . . .
vo ist

it's not . . .
es ist nicht . . .
ess ist nisht

is it . . .?
ist es . . .?
ist ess

is there . . . here?
gibt es hier . . .?
geept ess heer

could you say that again?
könnten Sie das noch einmal wiederholen?
kurnten zee dass nok inmal veederhohlen

please don't speak so fast
sprechen Sie bitte nicht so schnell
shpreshen zee bittuh nisht zo shnell

I don't understand
ich verstehe nicht
ish fairshtay-uh nisht

9

GENERAL PHRASES

OK
okay
okay

come on, let's go!
gehen wir!
gay-en veer

what's that in German?
wie heißt das auf deutsch?
vee hîst dass owf doytsh

that's fine!
das ist in Ordnung
dass ist in ortnoong

Abfälle	litter
Ausgang	way out
Auskunft	enquiries
außer Betrieb	out of order
besetzt	engaged
Betreten verboten	keep out
bitte nicht ...	please do not ...
Damen	ladies
Drücken	push
Eingang	way in
Eintritt frei	admission free
frisch gestrichen	wet paint
geöffnet	open
geschlossen	closed
Herren	gents
Kein Zutritt	no entry
links	left
Nicht ...	do not ...
Plakate ankleben verboten	stick no bills
rechts	right
verboten	forbidden
Ziehen	pull
Zu verkaufen	for sale

airport	der Flughafen *flookhahfen*
baggage	das Gepäck *gepeck*
book	reservieren *rezairveeren*
(*in advance*)	
coach	ein Bus *booss*
docks	die Docks *doks*
ferry	eine Fähre *fayruh*
gate	der Flugsteig *flookstīg*
(*at airport*)	
harbour	der Hafen *hahfen*
hovercraft	ein Luftkissenboot *looftkissenboht*
plane	ein Flugzeug *flooktsoyg*
sleeper	ein Liegewagen *leeguh-vahgen*
station	der Bahnhof *bahnhohf*
taxi	ein Taxi *taxi*
train	der Zug *tsook*

a ticket to . . .
eine Fahrkarte nach . . .
īnuh farkartuh nahκ

I'd like to reserve a seat
ich möchte gern einen Platz reservieren
ish murshtuh gairn īnen plats rezairveeren

smoking/non-smoking please
Raucher/Nichtraucher, bitte
rowκer/nisht-rowκer bittuh

a window seat please
einen Fensterplatz, bitte
īnen fensterplats bittuh

which platform is it for . . .?
von welchem Gleis fährt der Zug nach . . . ab?
fon velshem glīss fayrt dair tsook nahκ . . . ap

11

COMING AND GOING

what time is the next flight?
wann ist der nächste Flug?
van ist dair nexstuh flook

is this the right train for . . .?
ist dies der Zug nach . . .?
*ist deess dair tsook nah*ĸ

is this bus going to . . .?
fährt dieser Bus nach . . .?
*fayrt deezer booss nah*ĸ

is this seat free?
ist dieser Platz frei?
ist deezer plats frī

do I have to change (trains)?
muß ich umsteigen?
mooss ish oomshtīgen

is this the right stop for . . .?
ist dies die Haltestelle für . . .?
ist deess dee haltuh-shtelluh fewr

which terminal is it for . . .?
welches ist das Terminal für . . .?
velshess ist dass turminal fewr

is this ticket ok?
ist diese Fahrkarte gültig?
ist deezuh farkartuh gewltik

I want to change my ticket
ich möchte gern umbuchen
*ish murshtuh gairn oomboo*ĸen

thanks for a lovely stay
vielen Dank für Ihre Gastfreundschaft
feelen dank fewr eeruh gast-froynt-shafft

thanks very much for coming to meet me
vielen Dank, daß du mich abgeholt hast
feelen dank dass doo mish ap-gehohlt hast

well, here we are in . . .
so, das ist . . .
zo dass ist

12

COMING AND GOING

haben Sie etwas zu verzollen?
hahben zee etvass tsoo fairtsollen
do you have anything to declare?

öffnen Sie Ihren Koffer, bitte
urffnen zee eeren koffer bittuh
would you open this bag please?

Abfahrt	departure(s)
Ankunft	arrival(s)
Anschluß	connection
Ausgang	exit, gate
Auslandsflüge	international departures
Bahnhof	station
Bahnsteig	platform
Bitte anschnallen	fasten your seat belts
DB	West German Railways
D-Zug	express
Eingang	entrance
Entwerter	ticket stamping machine
Fahrkarten	tickets
Fahrplan	timetable
Flug	flight
Flughafen	airport
Flugsteig	gate
Gepäckausgabe	baggage claim
Gleis	platform
Handgepäck	hand luggage
Inlandsflüge	domestic departures
Nichtraucher	non-smoking
Raucher	smoking
S-Bahn	local railway
Verspätung	delay
Wartesaal	waiting room
Zoll	customs
Zu den Zügen	to the trains

bed	ein Bett *bett*
breakfast	das Frühstück *frewshtewk*
dinner	das Abendessen *ahbentessen*
dining room	das Speisezimmer *shpizuh-tsimmer*
double room	ein Doppelzimmer *doppel-tsimmer*
guesthouse	eine Pension *pens-yohn*
hotel	ein Hotel *hohtel*
key	der Schlüssel *shlewssel*
lunch	das Mittagessen *mittahk-essen*
night	eine Nacht *nahкt*
(in hotel)	eine Übernachtung *ewber-nahкtoong*
private bathroom	ein eigenes Bad *igeness baht*
reception	der Empfang *empfang*
room	ein Zimmer *tsimmer*
shower	eine Dusche *dOOshuh*
single room	ein Einzelzimmer *intsel-tsimmer*
with bath	mit Bad *mit baht*
youth hostel	eine Jugendherberge *yOOgent-hairbairguh*

do you have a room for one night?
ich hätte gern ein Zimmer für eine Nacht
ish hettuh gairn in tsimmer fewr inuh nahкt

do you have a room for one person?
haben Sie ein Einzelzimmer?
hahben zee in intsel-tsimmer

do you have a room for two people?
haben Sie ein Zweibettzimmer?
hahben zee in tsvibett-tsimmer

we'd like to rent a room for a week
wir möchten ein Zimmer für eine Woche mieten
veer murshten in tsimmer fewr inuh voкuh meeten

14

GETTING A ROOM

I'm looking for a good cheap room
ich suche ein gutes preiswertes Zimmer
ish zookuh in gootes priss-vairtess tsimmer

I have a reservation
ich habe ein Zimmer reserviert
ish hahbuh in tsimmer rezairveert

how much is it?
was kostet es?
vass kostet ess

can I see the room please?
kann ich das Zimmer sehen, bitte?
kan ish dass tsimmer zay-en bittuh

does that include breakfast?
ist das einschließlich Frühstück?
ist dass in-shleesslish frewshtewk

a room overlooking the Rhine
ein Zimmer mit Blick auf den Rhein
in tsimmer mit blick owf dayn rin

we'd like to stay another night
wir möchten gern noch einen Tag bleiben
veer murshten gairn nok inen tahk bliben

we will be arriving late
wir kommen erst spät an
veer kommen airst shpayt an

can I have my bill please?
können Sie meine Rechnung fertigmachen, bitte?
kurnen zee minuh reshnoong fairtik-mahken bittuh

I'll pay cash
ich zahle in bar
ish tsahluh in bar

can I pay by credit card?
kann ich mit Kreditkarte bezahlen?
kan ish mit kredeetkartuh betsahlen

will you give me a call at 6.30 in the morning?
können Sie mich um 6 Uhr 30 wecken?
kurnen zee mish oom zeks oor drissik vecken

GETTING A ROOM

at what time do you serve breakfast/dinner?
um wieviel Uhr wird das Frühstück/Abendessen
serviert?
*oom veefeel oor veert dass frewshtewk/ahbentessen
zairveert*

can we have breakfast in our room?
können wir auf unserem Zimmer frühstücken?
kurnen veer owf oonzerem tsimmer frewshtewken

thanks for putting us up
vielen Dank, daß Sie uns untergebracht haben
feelen dank dass zee oonss oontergebrahкt hahben

Aufzug	lift
Bad	bathroom
Bitte nicht stören	please do not disturb
Campingplatz	campsite
DJH	German Youth Hostel Association
Dusche	shower
Empfang	reception
Erdgeschoß	ground floor
Halbpension	half board
Jugendherberge	youth hostel
Notausgang	emergency exit
Nur für Gäste	for residents only
Pension	guesthouse
Souterrain	basement
Speisezimmer	dining room
Stock(werk)	floor
Übernachtung mit Frühstück	bed and breakfast
voll belegt	no vacancies
Vollpension	full board
Zimmer frei	vacancies
Zimmer zu vermieten	rooms to let
Zuschlag	surcharge

EATING OUT

bill	die Rechnung *reshnoong*
dessert	der Nachtisch *nahκtish*
drink	trinken *trinken*
eat	essen *essen*
food	das Essen *essen*
main course	das Hauptgericht *howptgerisht*
menu	die Speisekarte *shpīzuh-kartuh*
restaurant	ein Restaurant *restoron*
salad	ein Salat *zalaht*
service	die Bedienung *bedeenoong*
starter	die Vorspeise *for-shpīzuh*
tip	das Trinkgeld *trink-gelt*
waiter	der Kellner *kelner*
waitress	der Kellnerin *kelnerin*

a table for three, please
einen Tisch für drei Personen, bitte
īnen tish fewr drī pairzohnen bittuh

can I see the menu?
kann ich die Speisekarte haben?
kan ish dee shpīzuh-kartuh hahben

we'd like to order
wir möchten gern bestellen
veer murshten gairn beshtellen

what do you recommend?
was können Sie empfehlen?
vass kurnen zee empfaylen

I'd like ... please
ich hätte gern ...
ish hettuh gairn

waiter!
Herr Ober!
hair ohber

17

EATING OUT

waitress!
Fräulein!
froylin

could we have the bill, please?
können wir bitte die Rechnung haben?
kurnen veer bittuh dee reshnoong hahben

two white coffees please
zwei Kaffee mit Milch, bitte
tsvi kaffay mit milsh bittuh

that's for me
das ist für mich
dass ist fewr mish

some more bread please
bitte noch etwas Brot
bittuh noк etvass broht

a bottle of red/white wine please
eine Flasche Rotwein/Weißwein, bitte
inuh flashuh rohtvin/vissvin bittuh

where's the toilet, please?
wo ist die Toilette, bitte?
voh ist dee twalettuh bittuh

Damen	ladies
einschließlich 15% Bedienung	15% service charge included
Eiscafé	ice-cream parlour also selling (soft) drinks
Herren	gents
Menü	set menu
Schnellimbiß	snack bar
Speisekarte	menu
Tagesgericht	today's set menu
Tageskarte	menu of the day
Weinkarte	wine list
Wirtshaus	inn
Zum Mitnehmen	to take away

Apfelmus apple purée
Arme Ritter bread soaked in milk and egg then fried
Auflauf (baked) pudding or omelette
Aufschnitt sliced cold cuts

Balkansalat cabbage and pepper salad
Bauernfrühstück bacon and potato omelette
Bechamelkartoffeln sliced potatoes in creamy sauce
Beilagen side salads, vegetables
Bismarckhering filleted pickled herring
Blätterteig puff pastry
Blumenkohl cauliflower
Blutwurst black pudding
Bockwurst large frankfurter
Bohnen beans
Bouillon clear soup
Bouletten meat balls
Braten roast meat
Brathering (pickled) fried herring (*served cold*)
Bratkartoffeln fried potatoes
Bratwurst grilled pork sausage
Brot bread
Brötchen roll
Bückling smoked red herring
Buttercremetorte cream cake

Champignons mushrooms
Chinakohl Chinese leaves
Currywurst curried pork sausage

Deutsches Beefsteak mince, hamburger
Dicke Bohnen broad beans

Eier eggs
Eintopf stew

Eis   ice (cream)
Eisbein   knuckles of pork
Erbsen   peas
Erdbeertorte   strawberry gateau

Falscher Hase   meat loaf
Fasan   pheasant
Feldsalat   lamb's lettuce
Filet   fillet (steak)
Fisch   fish
Fischstäbchen   fish fingers
Fleischkäse   meat loaf
Fleischsalat   diced meat salad with mayonnaise
Fleischwurst   pork sausage
Forelle blau   trout au bleu (*boiled*)
Forelle Müllerin (Art)   trout with butter and lemon
   (*breaded*)
Frikadelle   rissole
Fruchtsaft   fruit juice
Frühlingsrolle   spring roll

Gänseleberpastete   goose liver pâté
Geflügel   poultry
Gekochter Schinken   boiled ham
Gemischter Salat   mixed salad
Gemüse   vegetable(s)
Geschnetzeltes   strips of meat in thick sauce
Gewürze   spices
Goldbarsch   type of perch
Götterspeise   jelly
Grüne Bohnen   French beans
Grünkohl   (curly) kale
Gurkensalat   cucumber salad

Hackfleisch   mince
Hähnchen   chicken
Hammelfleisch   mutton
Hasenpfeffer   jugged hare
Hauptgerichte   main dishes
Hausfrauenart   home-made-style
Heringssalat   herring salad

Himmel und Erde potato and apple purée with liver sausage/black pudding
Hoppelpoppel bacon and potato omelette
Hühnerfrikassee chicken fricassee
Hummer lobster

Jägerschnitzel pork with mushrooms

Kabeljau cod
Kaffee coffee
Kaiserschmarren sugared pancake with raisins
Kalbsschnitzel veal cutlet
Kalte Platte salad
Kaltschale cold sweet soup
Kaninchen rabbit
Kännchen pot
Karpfen carp
Kartoffelpuffer potato fritters
Käseplatte cheese board
Kasseler (Rippenspeer) smoked and salted (rib of) pork
Katenrauchwurst smoked sausage
Kieler Sprotten smoked sprats
Knackwurst frankfurter
Knoblauchbrot garlic bread
Knödel dumplings
Kohl cabbage
Kohlrouladen stuffed cabbage leaves
Königinpastete chicken vol-au-vent
Königsberger Klopse meatballs in caper sauce
Kopfsalat lettuce
Kotelett chop
Krabben shrimps/prawns
Kräutersauce herb sauce
Krautsalat coleslaw

Labskaus meat, fish and potato stew
Lachs salmon
Lammrücken saddle of lamb
Lauchsuppe leek soup
Leberkäse baked pork and beef loaf

Leberpastete liver pâté
Leipziger Allerlei mixed vegetables
Linseneintopf lentil stew

Makrele mackerel
Markklößchen marrow dumplings
Matjes(hering) young herring
Meeresfrüchte seafood
Meerrettichsauce horseradish sauce
Milch milk
Mineralwasser (sparkling) mineral water
Möhren, Mohrrüben carrots
Muscheln mussels

Nachspeisen desserts
Nierenragout kidney stew
Nudelsalat noodle salad

Ochsenschwanzsuppe oxtail soup

Palatschinken stuffed pancakes
Paprikaschoten peppers
Pastete vol-au-vent
Pellkartoffeln potatoes boiled in their jackets
Petersilienkartoffeln potatoes with parsley
Pfannkuchen pancake
Pfeffer pepper
Pfifferlinge chanterelles (*mushrooms*)
Pichelsteiner Topf vegetable stew with diced beef
Pilze mushrooms
Pökelfleisch salt meat
Pommes frites French fries
Porree leek
Potthast braised beef with sauce
Prinzeßbohnen unsliced runner beans
Püree (potato) purée
Putenschenkel leg of turkey

Quark curd cheese

Radieschen radishes

MENU READER

Räucherhering kipper, smoked herring
Reibekuchen potato waffles
Reissalat rice salad
Rinder(schmor)braten pot roast
Rindfleischsuppe beef broth
Rippchen spare rib
Risi-Pisi rice and peas
Rollmops rolled-up pickled herring, rollmops
Rosenkohl Brussels sprouts
Rostbraten roast
Rostbratwurst barbecued sausage
Röstkartoffeln fried potatoes
Rotbarsch type of perch
Rote Bete beetroot
Rote Grütze red fruit jelly
Rotkohl red cabbage
Rouladen beef olive
Rührei mit Speck scrambled egg with bacon
Russische Eier egg mayonnaise

Sahnesoße cream sauce
Salz salt
Salzheringe salted herrings
Salzkartoffeln boiled potatoes
Sauerbraten marinaded potroast
Sauerkraut white cabbage, finely chopped and
  pickled
Schaschlik (shish-)kebab
Schellfisch haddock
Schildkrötensuppe real turtle soup
Schillerlocken smoked haddock rolls
Schinkenröllchen rolled ham
Schlachtplatte selection of fresh sausages
Schmorbraten pot roast
Schnitzel cutlet
Scholle plaice
Schwarzwälder Kirschtorte Black Forest cherry
  gateau
Schwarzwurzeln salsifies
Schweinshaxe knuckle of pork
Seelachs pollack (*type of fish*)

MENU READER

Seezunge sole
Selleriesalat celery salad
Semmelknödel bread dumplings
Senfsauce mustard sauce
Serbisches Reisfleisch diced pork, onions, tomatoes
   and rice
Spanferkel sucking pig
Spargelcremesuppe cream of asparagus soup
Spätzle home-made noodles
Speck bacon
Spiegeleier fried eggs
Spießbraten joint roasted on a spit
Spinat spinach
Stollen type of fruit loaf
Streuselkuchen sponge cake with crumble topping
Suppe soup
Szegediner Gulasch goulash with pickled cabbage

Tee   tea
Thunfisch tuna

Ungarischer Gulasch Hungarian goulash

Verlorene Eier poached eggs
Vom Rind/Schwein/Lamm beef/pork/lamb
Vorspeisen starters

Waldorfsalat salad with celery, apples and walnuts
Weißkohl white cabbage
Weißwurst veal sausage
Wiener Schnitzel veal in breadcrumbs
Wild   game
Wirsing savoy cabbage
Würstchen frankfurter
Wurstplatte selection of sausages

Zigeunerschnitzel pork with peppers and relishes
Zucchini courgettes
Zucker sugar
Zuckererbsen mange-tout peas
Zungenragout tongue stew
Zwiebeltorte onion tart

HAVING A DRINK

bar	eine Bar *bar*
beer	ein Bier *beer*
coke (R)	eine Cola *kola*
dry	trocken *trocken*
fresh orange	ein Orangensaft *oronJen-zaft*
gin and tonic	ein Gin Tonic *djin-tonik*
ice	das Eis *īss*
lager	ein helles Bier *helles beer*
lemonade	eine Limonade *leemonahduh*
pub	eine Kneipe *k-nīpuh*
red	rot *roht*
straight	pur *poor*
sweet	süß *sewss*
vodka	ein Wodka *votka*
whisky	ein Whisky *viskee*
white	weiß *vīss*
wine	der Wein *vīn*

let's go for a drink
komm, wir gehen einen trinken
kom veer gay-en īnen trinken

a beer please
ein Bier, bitte
īn beer bittuh

two beers please
zwei Bier, bitte
tsvī beer bittuh

a glass of red/white wine
ein Glas Rotwein/Weißwein
īn glahss rohtvīn/vīssvīn

with lots of ice
mit viel Eis
mit feel īss

HAVING A DRINK

no ice thanks
ohne Eis, bitte
ohnuh īss bittuh

can I have another one?
bitte noch eins
bittuh noκ īnss

the same again please
dasselbe nochmal, bitte
dasselbuh noκmal bittuh

what'll you have?
was möchtest du/möchten Sie?
vass murshtest doo/murshten zee

I'll get this round
das ist meine Runde
dass ist mīnuh roonduh

not for me thanks
danke, nicht für mich
dankuh nisht fewr mish

he's absolutely smashed
er ist total besoffen
air ist tohtahl bezoffen

Alsterwasser	shandy
Alt(bier)	light brown beer, not sweet
Gespritzer	wine and soda, spritzer
Helles	like lager
Korn	type of schnapps
Maß	Bavarian word for a litre of beer
Mineralwasser	mineral water
Radler(maß)	shandy
Rotwein	red wine
vom Faß	draught
Weißwein	white wine

26

COLLOQUIAL EXPRESSIONS

barmy	bescheuert *beshoyert*
bastard	Arschloch *arshlok*
bloke	ein Typ *tewp*
boozer (*pub*)	eine Kneipe *k-nīpuh*
nutter	ein Verrückter *fair-rewkter*
pissed	besoffen *bezoffen*
thickie; twit	ein Blödmann *blurtman*

great!
toll!
toll

that's awful!
das ist furchtbar!
dass ist foorshtbar

shut up!
halt den Mund!
halt dayn moont

ouch!
au!
ow

yum-yum!
mmmh!
mmm

I'm absolutely knackered
ich bin völlig fertig
ish bin furlik fairtik

I'm fed up
mir reicht's
meer rīshts

I'm fed up with . . .
ich habe die Nase voll von . . .
ish hahbuh dee nahzuh foll von

COLLOQUIAL EXPRESSIONS

don't make me laugh!
daß ich nicht lache!
dass ish nisht lahкe

you've got to be joking!
du machst wohl Witze!
doo mahкst vohl vitsuh

it's rubbish (*goods etc*)
das ist Mist!
dass ist mist

it's a rip-off
das ist Wucher!
dass ist vooкer

get lost!
verschwinde!
fairshvinduh

it's a damn nuisance
das ist verdammt ärgerlich
dass ist fairdamt airgerlish

I don't believe it!
das gibt's doch nicht!
dass geepts doк nisht

du liebe Zeit!	struth!
keine Ahnung	no idea
klar	ok, sure thing
mach schon!	get on with it!
mach's gut	take care
Mensch!	*expresses amazement, annoyance etc*
Sonntagsfahrer!	learn to drive!
stark	great
tschüs	cheerio

GETTING AROUND

bike	ein Fahrrad *far-raht*
bus	ein Bus *booss*
car	ein Auto *owto*
change (*trains*)	umsteigen *oomshtīgen*
garage (*for fuel*)	eine Tankstelle *tank-shtelluh*
hitch-hike	trampen *trempen*
map	eine Landkarte *lantkartuh*
motorbike	ein Motorrad *mohtor-raht*
petrol	das Benzin *bentseen*
return (ticket)	eine Rückfahrkarte *rewk-farkartuh*
single	eine einfache Fahrkarte *īnfahкuh farkartuh*
station	der Bahnhof *bahnhof*
taxi	ein Taxi *taxi*
ticket	eine Fahrkarte *farkartuh*
train	ein Zug *tsook*
underground	die U-Bahn *OO-bahn*

I'd like to rent a car/bike
ich möchte gern ein Auto/ein Fahrrad mieten
ish murshtuh gairn īn owto/īn far-raht meeten

how much is it per day?
was kostet es pro Tag?
vass kostet ess pro tahk

when do I have to bring the car back?
bis wann muß ich das Auto zurückbringen?
biss van mooss ish dass owto tsoorewk-bring-en

I'm heading for ...
ich bin auf dem Weg nach ...
ish bin owf daym vayk nahк

how do I get to ...?
wie komme ich nach ...?
vee kommuh ish nahк

29

GETTING AROUND

REPLIES

geradeaus
gerahduh-owss
straight on

links/rechts abbiegen
links/reshts ap-beegen
turn left/right

es ist das Gebäude dort
ess ist dass geboyduh dort
it's that building there

gehen/fahren Sie zurück bis zur . . .
gay-en/faren zee tsoorewk biss tsoor
go back as far as the . . .

die erste/zweite/dritte Straße links
dee airstuh/tsvītuh/drittuh shtrahssuh links
first/second/third on the left

we're just travelling around
wir sehen uns in der Gegend um
veer zay-en oonss in dair gaygent oom

I'm a stranger here
ich bin fremd hier
ish bin fremt heer

is that on the way?
liegt das auf dem Weg?
leegt dass owf daym vayk

can I get off here?
kann ich hier aussteigen?
kan ish heer owss-shtīgen

thanks very much for the lift
danke fürs Mitnehmen
dankuh fewrss mitnaymen

two returns to . . . please
zwei Rückfahrkarten nach . . . bitte
tsvī rewk-farkarten nahк . . . bittuh

GETTING AROUND

what time is the last train back?
wann fährt der letzte Zug zurück?
van fayrt dair letstuh tsook tsoorewk

we want to leave tomorrow and come back the day after
wir möchten morgen abreisen und am folgenden Tag wiederkommen
veer murshten morgen ap-rīzen oont am folgenden tahk veederkommen

we're coming back the same day
wir kommen am gleichen Tag zurück
veer kommen am glīshen tahk tsoorewk

is this the right platform for . . .?
ist dies der Bahnsteig für Züge nach . . .?
ist deess dair bahnshtī k fewr tsewguh nahk

is this train going to . . .?
fährt dieser Zug nach . . .?
fayrt deezer tsook nahk

which station is this?
wo sind wir hier?
vo zint veer heer

which stop is it for . . .?
welches ist die Haltestelle für . . .
velshess ist dee haltuh-shtelluh fewr

is there any sort of runabout ticket?
gibt es eine Karte für Rundreisen?
geept ess īnuh kartuh fewr roontrīzen

can I take my bike on the train?
kann ich mein Fahrrad im Zug mitführen?
kan ish mīn far-raht im tsook mit-fewren

how far is it to the nearest petrol station?
wie weit ist es bis zur nächsten Tankstelle?
vee vīt ist ess biss tsoor nexsten tank-shtelluh

I need a new tyre
ich brauche einen neuen Reifen
ish browkuh īnen noyen rīfen

GETTING AROUND

it's overheating
der Motor läuft heiß
dair mohtor loyft hīss

there's something wrong with the brakes
mit den Bremsen stimmt etwas nicht
mit dayn bremzen shtimmt etvass nisht

Abfahrt	departure(s)
Ankunft	arrival(s)
Anlieger frei	residents only
Ausfahrt	exit
Bahnsteig	platform
bitte entwerten	please stamp your ticket
bleifrei	unleaded
D-Zug	express
Eilzug	fast local train
Entwerter	ticket stamping machine
Fahrkartenautomat	ticket machine
Gleis	platform
Haltestelle	stop
Halteverbot	no stopping
Mißbrauch strafbar	penalty for misuse
Monatskarte	monthly season ticket
Nahverkehrszug	local train
Netzkarte	runabout ticket
Nicht hinauslehnen	do not lean out
Normal	two-star
Notbremse	emergency brake
Parken verboten	no parking
SB-Tankstelle	self-service
Schnellzug	express
Straßenbauarbeiten	roadworks
Super	four-star
Tankstelle	petrol station
U-Bahn	underground
Umleitung	diversion
Vorfahrt gewähren	give way
Wochenkarte	weekly ticket

carrier bag	eine Tragetasche *trahguh-tashuh*
cashdesk	die Kasse *kassuh*
cheap	preiswert *prīss-vairt*
cheque	ein Scheck *sheck*
department	die Abteilung *aptīloong*
expensive	teuer *toyer*
pay	bezahlen *betsahlen*
receipt	eine Quittung *kvittoong*
shop	ein Geschäft *gesheft*
shop assistant	ein(e) Verkäufer(in) *fairkoyfer(in)*
supermarket	ein Supermarkt *zOOpermarkt*
till	die Kasse *kassuh*

I'd like ...
ich möchte gern ...
ish murshtuh gairn

have you got ...?
haben Sie ...?
hahben zee

can I just have a look around?
kann ich mich nur mal umsehen?
kan ish mish nOOr mal oomzay-en

how much is this?
was kostet das?
vass kostet dass

the one in the window
der/die/das im Schaufenster
dair/dee/dass im showfenster

do you take credit cards?
akzeptieren Sie Kreditkarten?
aktsepteeren zee kredeetkarten

33

SHOPPING

could I have a receipt please?
kann ich bitte eine Quittung haben?
kan ish bittuh inuh kvittoong hahben

I'd like to try it on
ich möchte es gern anprobieren
ish murshtuh es gairn anprobeeren

I'll come back
ich komme noch einmal wieder
ish kommuh nok inmal veeder

it's too big/small
es ist zu groß/klein
ess ist tsoo grohss/klin

it's not what I'm looking for
es ist nicht das, was ich möchte
ess ist nisht dass vass ish murshtuh

I'll take it
ich nehme es
ish naymuh ess

can you gift-wrap it?
können Sie es als Geschenk einpacken?
kurnen zee ess alss geshenk inpacken

Abteilung	department
Geschlossen	closed
Haltbar bis ...	best before ...
Kasse	cash point
Kühl lagern	keep in a cool place
Öffnungszeiten	opening times
Preissenkung	reduction
Sommerschlußverkauf	summer sales
Sonderangebot	special offer
Winterschlußverkauf	winter sales
Zum baldigen Verbrauch bestimmt	will not keep
zweite Wahl	seconds

GERMANY AND THINGS GERMAN

Some names (in German-speaking countries) which are different in German:

Bavaria	Bayern *bī-ern*
Cologne	Köln *kurln*
Danube	die Donau *dohnow*
Geneva	Genf *genf*
Lake Constance	der Bodensee *bohdenzay*
Lake Lucerne	Vierwaldstätter See *veervalt-shtetter zay*
Munich	München *mewnshen*
Rhine	der Rhein *rīn*
Vienna	Wien *veen*
die Altstadt	old (part of) town
die BRD	(Bundesrepublik Deutschland) FRG
die DDR	(Deutsche Demokratische Republik) GDR
Fasching, Karneval	annual carnival held in the pre-Lent period with fancy-dress processions and general celebrating
die Länder	the eleven adminstrative districts of West Germany
die Mauer	the (Berlin) wall
das Oktoberfest	annual Munich beer festival (starting in September)
das Rathaus	town hall
der Rosenmontagszug	main, locally organized, procession of 'Fasching', held on the Monday before Ash Wednesday.
das Schloß	castle
der Schwarzwald	Black Forest
der Tag der Deutschen Einheit	Day of German Unity, 17th June, a public holiday
die Waterkant	North German name for the North German coastal area
die Weinstraße	route through wine-growing areas

bank	eine Bank *bank*
bill	die Rechnung *reshnoong*
bureau de change	eine Wechselstube *veksel-shtoobuh*
cash dispenser	ein Geldautomat *gelt-owtomaht*
change (*small*)	das Kleingeld *klin-gelt*
cheque	ein Scheck *sheck*
credit card	eine Kreditkarte *kredeetkartuh*
Eurocheque	ein Euroscheck *oyrosheck*
exchange rate	der Wechselkurs *vekselkoorss*
expensive	teuer *toyer*
German marks	D-Mark *day-mark*
pounds (sterling)	(englische) Pfund *(eng-lishuh) pfoont*
price	der Preis *priss*
receipt	die Quittung *kvittoong*
traveller's cheque	ein Reisescheck *rizuh-sheck*

how much is it?
was kostet es?
vass kostet ess

I'd like to change this into . . .
ich möchte dies in . . . umtauschen
ich murshtuh deess in . . . oom-towshen

can you give me something smaller for this?
können Sie mir das wechseln?
kurnen zee meer dass vekseln

can I use this credit card?
akzeptieren Sie diese Kreditkarte?
aktsepteeren zee deezuh kredeetkartuh

can we have the bill please?
wir hätten gern die Rechnung
veer hetten gairn dee reshnoong

MONEY

please keep the change
der Rest ist für Sie
dair rest ist fewr zee

does that include service?
ist das einschließlich Bedienung?
ist dass inshleesslish bedeenoong

what are your rates?
was sind Ihre Preise?
vass zint eeruh prīzuh

I think the figures are wrong
ich glaube hier stimmt etwas nicht
ish glowbuh heer shtimmt etvass nisht

I'm completely skint
ich bin völlig pleite
ish bin furlik plītuh

The unit is the 'Mark', which is divided into 100 'Pfennige'. A 'Groschen' is a ten pfennig piece. The Germans do not refer to the currency as 'Deutschmarks' — this is an English invention only.

Ausländische Währungen	foreign currencies
Bank	bank
Bargeld	cash
Brief	selling rate
Euroscheck	Eurocheque
Geld	buying rate
Kreditkarte	credit card
MWSt	VAT
Pfund	pound
Reisescheck	traveller's cheque
Scheckkarte	cheque card
Sparkasse	savings bank
Wechsel(stube)	bureau de change
Wechselkurs	exchange rate

band (*pop*)	eine Band *bant*
cinema	das Kino *keeno*
concert	ein Konzert *kontsairt*
disco	eine Diskothek *diskotayk*
film	ein Film *film*
go out	ausgehen *owss-gay-en*
music	die Musik *moozeek*
play (*theatre*)	ein Stück *shtewk*
seat	ein Platz *plats*
show	eine Vorstellung *for-shtelloong*
singer	ein(e) Sänger(in) *zeng-er(in)*
theatre	das Theater *tay-ahter*
ticket	eine Eintrittskarte *intritts-kartuh*

are you doing anything tonight?
hast du/haben Sie heute abend etwas vor?
hast doo/hahben zee hoytuh ahbent etvass for

do you want to come out with me?
sollen wir zusammen ausgehen?
zollen veer tsoozammen owss-gay-en

what's on?
was läuft?
vass loyft

have you got a programme of what's on in town?
haben Sie ein Veranstaltungsprogramm für die Stadt?
hahben zee in fairanshtaltoongs-program fewr dee shtat

which is the best disco round here?
welches ist hier die beste Diskothek?
velshess ist heer dee bestuh diskotayk

let's go to the cinema/theatre
laß uns ins Kino/Theater gehen
lass oonss inss keeno/tay-ahter gay-en

ENTERTAINMENT

I've seen it
das habe ich schon gesehen
dass hahbuh ish shohn gezay-en

I'll meet you at 9 o'clock at the station
wir treffen uns um 9 Uhr am Bahnhof
veer treffen oonss oom noyn oor am bahnhohf

can I have two tickets for tonight?
ich hätte gern zwei Karten für heute abend
ish hettuh gairn tsvī karten fewr hoytuh ahbent

do you want to dance?
möchtest du tanzen?
murshtest doo tantsen

thanks but I'm with my boyfriend
danke, aber ich bin mit meinem Freund hier
dankuh ahber ish bin mit mīnem froynt heer

let's go out for some fresh air
komm, wir gehen ein bißchen an die frische Luft
kom veer gay-en īn biss-shen an dee frishuh looft

will you let me back in again later?
kann ich später wiederkommen?
kan ish shpayter veederkommen

I'm meeting someone inside
ich treffe mich drinnen mit jemandem
ish treffuh mish drinnen mit yaymandem

ausverkauft	sold out
Garderobe	cloakroom
Geschlossen	closed
Kasse	box office
mit Untertiteln	with subtitles
Nächste Vorstellung um . . .	next performance at . . .
Parkett	stalls
Pause	interval

beach	der Strand *shtrant*
bikini	ein Bikini *beekeenee*
dive	tauchen *towken*
sand	der Sand *zant*
sea	das Meer *mayr*
sunbathe	sonnenbaden *zonnenbahden*
suntan lotion	die Sonnencreme *zonnenkraym*
suntan oil	das Sonnenöl *zonnenurl*
swim	schwimmen *shvimmen*
swimming	der Badeanzug
costume	*bahduh-antsook*
tan (*verb*)	(sich) bräunen *(zish) broynen*
towel	ein Badetuch *bahduh-took*
wave	eine Welle *velluh*

let's go to the beach/pool
komm, gehen wir zum Strand/Schwimmbad
kom gay-en veer tsoom shtrant/shvimmbaht

what's the water like?
wie ist es im Wasser?
vee ist ess im vasser

it's freezing
es ist eiskalt
ess ist īsskalt

it's beautiful
es ist schön
ess ist shurn

are you coming for a swim?
kommst du mit schwimmen?
kommst doo mit shvimmen

I can't swim
ich kann nicht schwimmen
ish kan nisht shvimmen

40

THE BEACH, THE POOL

he swims like a fish
er schwimmt wie ein Fisch
air shvimmt vee in fish

will you keep an eye on my things for me?
könnten Sie auf meine Sachen aufpassen?
kurnten zee owf minuh zahken owfpassen

is it deep here?
ist das Wasser hier tief?
ist dass vasser heer teef

could you rub suntan oil on my back?
kannst du meinen Rücken mit Sonnenöl einreiben?
kanst doo minen rewken mit zonnenurl inriben

I love sun bathing
ich liebe Sonnenbaden
ish leebuh zonnenbahden

I'm all sunburnt
ich habe einen totalen Sonnenbrand
ish hahbuh inen tohtahlen zonnenbrant

you're all wet!
du bist ganz naß!
doo bist gants nass

DLRG	lifeguards
Duschen	showers
Ebbe/Flut	low tide/high tide
Eis	ice cream
Freibad	open-air pool
Gefährliche Strömung	dangerous current
Rettungsring	lifebelt
Schwimmen verboten	no swimming
Strandkorb	wickerwork, high-backed beach chair
zu vermieten	for hire

accident	ein Unfall *oonfal*
ambulance	ein Krankenwagen *krankenvahgen*
broken	gebrochen *gebroкen*
doctor	ein Arzt *artst*
emergency	ein Notfall *nohtfal*
fire	ein Feuer *foy-er*
fire brigade	die Feuerwehr *foy-er-vayr*
ill	krank *krank*
injured	verletzt *fairletst*
late	zu spät *tsoo shpayt*
(train, bus etc)	verspätet *fairshpaytet*
out of order	außer Betrieb *owsser betreep*
police	die Polizei *politsī*

can you help me? I'm lost
können Sie mir helfen? ich weiß nicht, wo ich bin
kurnen zee meer helfen — ish vīss nisht vo ish bin

I've lost my passport
ich habe meinen Paß verloren
ish hahbuh mīnen pas fairloren

I've locked myself out of my room
ich habe mich ausgesperrt
ish hahbuh mish owss-geshpairt

my luggage hasn't arrived
mein Gepäck ist noch nicht angekommen
mīn gepeck ist noк nisht angekommen

I can't get it open
ich bekomme es nicht auf
ish bekomme ess nisht owf

it's jammed
es klemmt
ess klemmt

PROBLEMS

I don't have enough money
ich habe nicht genug Geld
ish hahbuh nisht genOOk gelt

I've broken down
ich habe eine Panne
ish hahbuh inuh pannuh

can I use your telephone please, this is an emergency
kann ich bitte Ihr Telefon benutzen, es ist ein Notfall
kan ish bittuh eer telefohn benootsen ess ist in nohtfal

help!
Hilfe!
hilfuh

it doesn't work
es funktioniert nicht
ess foonkt-syohneert nisht

the lights aren't working in my room
das Licht in meinem Zimmer funktioniert nicht
dass lisht in minem tsimmer foonkt-syohneert nisht

the lift is stuck
der Fahrstuhl ist steckengeblieben
dair farshtool ist shtecken-gebleeben

I can't understand a single word
ich verstehe kein Wort
ish fairshtayuh kin vort

can you get an interpreter?
können Sie einen Dolmetscher besorgen?
kurnen zee inen dolmetsher bezorgen

the toilet won't flush
die Spülung der Toilette funktioniert nicht
dee shpewloong dair tvalettuh foonkt-syohneert nisht

there's no plug in the bath
es ist kein Stöpsel in der Badewanne
ess ist kin shturpsel in dair bahduh-vannuh

there's no hot water
es gibt kein warmes Wasser
ess geept kin varmess vasser

PROBLEMS

there's no toilet paper left
das Toilettenpapier ist alle
dass twaletten-papeer ist aluh

I'm afraid I've accidentally broken the . . .
mir ist leider aus Versehen der/die/das . . .
kaputtgegangen
meer ist lider owss fairzay-en dair/dee/dass . . .
kapoot-ge-gang-en

this man has been following me
dieser Mann folgt mir ständig
deezer man folgt meer shtendik

I've been mugged
ich bin überfallen worden
ish bin ewberfal-en vorden

my handbag has been stolen
meine Handtasche ist gestohlen worden
minuh hant-tashuh ist geshtohlen vorden

Achtung	beware, attention
Außer Betrieb	out of order
Betreten auf eigene Gefahr	enter at own risk, keep off/out
Betreten verboten	keep out
Defekt	faulty
Feuerwehr	fire brigade
Fundbüro	lost property office
Nicht . . .	do not . . .
Notausgang	emergency exit
Notruf	emergency call
(strengstens) untersagt	(strictly) prohibited
verboten	forbidden
Vorsicht bissiger Hund	beware of the dog
Vorsicht Stufe!	mind the step

bandage	der Verband *fairbant*
blood	das Blut *bloot*
broken	gebrochen *gebroken*
burn	die Verbrennung *fairbrennoong*
chemist's	die Apotheke *apotaykuh*
contraception	die Empfängnisverhütung *empfengniss-fairhewtoong*
dentist	ein Zahnarzt *tsahnartst*
disabled	behindert *behindert*
disease	eine Krankheit *krankhīt*
doctor	ein Arzt *artst*
health	die Gesundheit *gezoonthīt*
hospital	ein Krankenhaus *krankenhowss*
ill	krank *krank*
nurse	eine Krankenschwester *krankenshvester*
wound	eine Wunde *voonduh*

I don't feel well
mir ist nicht gut
meer ist nisht goot

it's getting worse
es wird schlimmer
ess veert shlimmer

I feel better
es geht mir besser
ess gayt meer besser

I feel sick
mir ist schlecht
meer ist shlesht

I've got a pain here
ich habe hier Schmerzen
ish hahbuh heer shmairtsen

HEALTH

it hurts
es tut weh
ess toot vay

could you call a doctor?
könnten Sie einen Arzt rufen?
kurnten zee inen artst rOOfen

is it serious?
ist es ernst?
ist ess airnst

will he need an operation?
muß er operiert werden?
mooss air opereert vairden

I'm diabetic
ich bin Diabetiker(in)
ish bin dee-abaytiker(in)

have you got anything for . . .?
haben Sie etwas gegen . . .?
hahben zee etvass gaygen

äußerlich anzuwenden	not to be taken internally
Beruhigungsmittel	tranquillizer
Nüchtern einzunehmen	to be taken on an empty stomach
Praktischer Arzt	GP
Praxis	doctor's surgery
rezeptpflichtig	sold on prescription only
Schlaftablette	sleeping pill
Schmerzmittel	painkiller
Sprechstunde	surgery
täglich	daily
Unfallstation	casualty ward
Vor Gebrauch schütteln	shake before use
Vor/nach den Mahlzeiten einzunehmen	to be taken before/ after meals

can we use the tennis court?
können wir den Tennisplatz benutzen?
kurnen veer dayn tennisplats benootsen

see you at the top of the skilift
wir sehen uns oben am Skilift
veer zay-en oonss ohben am sheelift

how much is a skipass?
was kostet ein Skipaß?
vass kostet īn sheepas

I'd like to go and watch a football match
ich möchte gern zu einem Fußballspiel gehen
ish murshtuh gairn tsoo īnem fOOssbal-shpeel gay-en

is it possible to do any horse-riding here?
gibt es hier Reitmöglichkeiten?
geept ess heer rīt-murglishkīten

we're going to do some hill-walking
wir werden etwas Bergwandern
veer vairden etvass bairk-vandern

we're on a mountaineering trip
wir sind zum Bergsteigen hier
veer zint tsoom bairk-shtīgen heer

I want to learn to sailboard
ich möchte gern Windsurfen lernen
ish murshtuh gairn vintzurfen lairnen

can we hire a sailing boat?
können wir ein Segelboot mieten?
kurnen veer īn zaygelboht meeten

this is the first time I've ever tried it
ich mache es zum ersten Mal
ish mahкuh ess tsoom airsten mahl

letter	der Brief *breef*
post office	die Post *posst*
recorded delivery	per Einschreiben *pair ĩnshrĩben*
send	senden *zenden*
stamp	eine Briefmarke *breefmarkuh*

how much is a letter to Ireland?
was ist das Porto für einen Brief nach Irland?
vass ist dass porto fewr ĩnen breef nahк eerlant

I'd like four 80 pfennig stamps
ich hätte gern vier Briefmarken zu 80 Pfennig
ish hettuh gairn feer breefmarken tsoo ahкtsik pfennik

I'd like six stamps for postcards to England
ich hätte gern sechs Marken für Postkarten nach
England
*ish hettuh gairn zeks marken fewr posstkarten nahк
eng-lant*

is there any mail for me?
ist Post für mich da?
ist posst fewr mish da

I'm expecting a parcel from London
ich erwarte ein Paket aus London
ish airvartuh ĩn pakayt owss london

Absender	sender
BP, Bundespost	German Post Office
Nächste Leerung	next collection
Einschreiben	registered mail
Postleitzahl	post code
Postwertzeichen in kleinen Mengen	stamps in small quantities

directory enquiries	die Auskunft *owsskoonft*
engaged	besetzt *bezetst*
extension	der Anschluß *anshlooss*
number	die Nummer *noommer*
operator	die Vermittlung *fairmittloong*
phone (verb)	telefonieren *telefohneeren*
phone box	eine Telefonzelle *telefohn-tselluh*
telephone	das Telefon *telefohn*
telephone directory	das Telefonbuch *telefohnbook*

is there a phone round here?
gibt es hier ein Telefon?
geept ess heer in telefohn

can I use your phone?
kann ich Ihr Telefon benutzen?
kan ish eer telefohn benootsen

I'd like to make a phone call to Britain
ich möchte gern nach Großbritannien telefonieren
ish murshtuh gairn nahk grohss-britanee-en telefohneeren

I want to reverse the charges
ich möchte ein R-Gespräch führen
ish murshtuh in air-geshpraysh fewren

hello, this is Simon speaking
hallo, hier ist Simon
hallo heer ist 'simon'

could I speak to Anna?
kann ich Anna sprechen?
kan ish 'anna' shpreshen

can I leave a message?
kann ich eine Nachricht hinterlassen?
kan ish inuh nahkrisht hinterlassen

TELEPHONING

do you speak English?
sprechen Sie englisch?
shpreshen zee eng-lish

could you say that again very very slowly?
könnten Sie das bitte noch einmal ganz langsam
wiederholen?
*kurnten zee dass bittuh nok inmal gants langzahm
veederhohlen*

could you tell him Jim called?
könnten Sie ihm sagen, daß Jim angerufen hat?
kurnten zee eem zahgen dass 'jim' angeroofen hat

could you ask her to ring me back?
könnten Sie sie bitten, mich zurückzurufen?
kurnten zee zee bitten mish tsoorewktsooroofen

I'll call back later
ich rufe später noch einmal an
ish roofuh shpayter nok inmal an

my number is . . .
meine Nummer ist . . .
minuh noomer ist . . .

76 32 11
sechsundsiebzig zweiunddreißig elf
zeks-oont-zeeptsik tsvi-oont-drisik elf

just a minute please
einen Augenblick, bitte
inen owgenblick bittuh

he's not in
er ist nicht da
air ist nisht da

sorry, I've got the wrong number
tut mir leid, ich habe mich verwählt
toot meer lit ish hahbuh mish fairvaylt

it's a terrible line
die Verbindung ist sehr schlecht
dee fairbindoong ist zair shlesht

TELEPHONING

REPLIES

bleiben Sie am Apparat
blīben zee am aparaht
hang on

wer spricht, bitte?
vair shprisht bittuh
who's calling?

am Apparat
am aparaht
speaking

Auf Wiederhören	goodbye
Auskunft	directory enquiries
Auslandsgespräch	international call
besetzt	engaged
Geld einwerfen	insert money
Ferngespräch	long distance call
Fernsprecher	telephone
Feuerwehr	fire brigade
Freizeichen	ringing tone
Großbritannien	UK
Hörer abnehmen	lift receiver
Hörer einhängen	replace receiver
Notruf (110)	emergencies
Ortsgespräch	local call
Telefonbuch	phone book
wählen	dial

THE ALPHABET

how do you spell it?
wie schreibt man das?
vee shrīpt man dass

I'll spell it
das schreibt man so: . . .
dass shrīpt man zo

a *ah*	g *gay*	m *em*	s *ess*	y *ewpsilon*
b *bay*	h *hah*	n *en*	t *tay*	z *tset*
c *tsay*	i *ee*	o *o*	u *oo*	
d *day*	j *yot*	p *pay*	v *fow*	
e *ay*	k *ka*	q *koo*	w *vay*	
f *ef*	l *el*	r *air*	x *eeks*	

NUMBERS, THE DATE AND THE TIME

0	null *nool*
1	eins *īnss*
2	zwei *tsvī*
3	drei *drī*
4	vier *feer*
5	fünf *fewnf*
6	sechs *zeks*
7	sieben *zeeben*
8	acht *ahκt*
9	neun *noyn*
10	zehn *tsayn*
11	elf *elf*
12	zwölf *tsvurlf*
13	dreizehn *drī-tsayn*
14	vierzehn *feer-tsayn*
15	fünfzehn *fewnf-tsayn*
16	sechzehn *zesh-tsayn*
17	siebzehn *zeep-tsayn*
18	achtzehn *ahκt-tsayn*
19	neunzehn *noyn-tsayn*
20	zwanzig *tsvantsik*
21	einundzwanzig *īn-oont-tsvantsik*
22	zweiundzwanzig *tsvī-oont-tsvantsik*
30	dreißig *drīssik*
35	fünfunddreißig *fewnf-oont-drīssik*
40	vierzig *feertsik*
50	fünfzig *fewnftsik*
60	sechzig *zeshtsik*
70	siebzig *zeeptsik*
80	achtzig *ahκtsik*
90	neunzig *noyntsik*
100	(ein)hundert *(īn)hoondert*
101	(ein)hundert(und)eins *(īn)hoondert(oont)īnss*

NUMBERS, THE DATE, THE TIME

200	zweihundert	*tsvīhoondert*
202	zweihundert(und)zwei	*tsvīhoondert(oont)tsvī*
1,000	(ein)tausend	*(īn)towzent*
2,000	zweitausend	*tsvītowzent*
1,000,000	eine Million	*mil-yohn*
1,000,000,000	eine Milliarde	*mil-yarduh*
1st	erste	*airstuh*
2nd	zweite	*tsvītuh*
3rd	dritte	*drittuh*
4th	vierte	*feertuh*
5th	fünfte	*fewnftuh*
6th	sechste	*zekstuh*
7th	siebte	*zeeptuh*
8th	achte	*ahᴋtuh*
9th	neunte	*noyntuh*
10th	zehnte	*tsayntuh*

two point five
zwei Komma fünf
tsvī komma fewnf

what's the date?
den wievielten haben wir heute?
dayn veefeelten hahben veer hoytuh

it's the first of June
es ist der erste Juni
ess ist dair airstuh yOOnee

it's the tenth/twelfth of May 1994
es ist der 10./12. Mai
neunzehnhundertvierundneunzig
ess ist dair tsayntuh/tsvurlftuh mī noyntsayn-hoondert-veer-oont-noyntsik

what time is it?
wie spät ist es?
vee shpayt ist ess

it's midday/midnight
es ist Mittag/Mitternacht
ess ist mittahк/mitternahкt

it's one/three/twelve o'clock
es ist ein Uhr/drei Uhr/zwölf Uhr
ess ist īn oor/drī oor/tsvurlf oor

it's twenty past three/twenty to three
es ist zwanzig nach drei/zwanzig vor drei
ess ist tsvantsik nahк drī/tsvantsik for drī

it's half past eight/ten
es ist halb neun/halb elf
ess ist halp noyn/halp elf

it's a quarter past five/a quarter to five
es ist Viertel nach fünf/Viertel vor fünf
ess ist feertel nahк fewnf/feertel for fewnf

it is 25 past eleven/25 to eleven
es ist fünf vor halb zwölf/fünf nach halb elf
ess ist fewnf for halp tsvurlf/fewnf nahк halp elf

at two/five p.m.
um vierzehn Uhr/siebzehn Uhr
oom feertsayn oor/zeeptsayn oor

a ein, eine, ein (*see grammar*)
about (*approx*) etwa
above über
abroad im Ausland; **go abroad** ins Ausland fahren
accelerator das Gaspedal
accent der Akzent
accept akzeptieren
accident der Unfall
accommodation die Unterkunft
accompany begleiten
ache der Schmerz
adaptor (*for voltage*) der Adapter; (*plug*) der Mehrfachstecker
address die Adresse
address book das Adreßbuch
adult der/die Erwachsene
advance: in advance im voraus
advise raten (*+dat*)
aeroplane das Flugzeug
afraid: I'm afraid (of) ich habe Angst (vor*+dat*)
after nach
afternoon der Nachmittag
aftershave das Rasierwasser
afterwards nachher
again nochmal
against gegen
age das Alter
agency die Agentur
agent der Vertreter

aggressive aggressiv
ago: three days ago vor drei Tagen
agree: I agree ich bin einverstanden
AIDS Aids
air die Luft
air-conditioned mit Klimaanlage
air-conditioning die Klimaanlage
air hostess die Stewardeß
airline die Fluglinie
airmail: by airmail per Luftpost
airport der Flughafen
alarm der Alarm
alarm clock der Wecker
alcohol der Alkohol
alive lebendig
all: all men/women alle Männer/Frauen; **all the milk/beer** alle Milch/alles Bier; **all day** den ganzen Tag; **that's all** das ist alles
allergic to allergisch gegen
all-inclusive inklusive
allow erlauben
allowed gestattet
all right: that's all right okay
almost fast
alone allein
Alps die Alpen *pl*
already schon
also auch
alternator die Lichtmaschine
although obwohl
altogether insgesamt

ENGLISH-GERMAN

always immer
a.m.: at 5 a.m. um 5 Uhr
  morgens
ambulance der
  Krankenwagen
America Amerika
American amerikanisch;
  (*man*) der Amerikaner;
  (*woman*) die Amerikanerin
among unter (*+acc*)
amp: 13-amp mit 13 Ampere
ancestor der Vorfahr
anchor der Anker
ancient uralt
and und
angina die Angina
angry böse
animal das Tier
ankle der Knöchel
anniversary (*wedding*) der
  Hochzeitstag
annoying ärgerlich
anorak der Anorak
another ein anderer, eine
  andere, ein anderes;
  another beer noch ein Bier
answer die Antwort
answer (*verb*) antworten
ant die Ameise
antibiotic das Antibiotikum
antifreeze das
  Frostschutzmittel
antihistamine das
  Antihistamin
antique: it's an antique es ist
  antik
antique shop der
  Antiquitätenladen
antiseptic das Antiseptikum
**any: have you got any butter/
  bananas?** haben Sie Butter/
  Bananen?; **I don't have
  any** ich habe keine

anyway sowieso
apartment das Zimmer
aperitif der Aperitif
apologize sich entschuldigen
appalling entsetzlich
appendicitis die
  Blinddarmentzündung
appetite der Appetit
apple der Apfel
apple pie der Apfelkuchen
appointment die
  Verabredung; (*with doctor*)
  der Termin
apricot die Aprikose
April der April
area die Gegend
arm der Arm
arrest festnehmen
arrival die Ankunft
arrive ankommen
art die Kunst
art gallery die Kunstgalerie
artificial künstlich
artist der Künstler
as (*since*) da; **as beautiful as**
  so schön wie
ashamed: to be ashamed sich
  schämen
ashtray der Aschenbecher
ask fragen
asleep: she's asleep sie
  schläft
asparagus der Spargel
aspirin das
  Kopfschmerzmittel
asthma das Asthma
astonishing erstaunlich
at: at the station am
  Bahnhof; **at Dagmar's** bei
  Dagmar; **at 3 o'clock** um 3
  Uhr
Atlantic der Atlantik
attractive attraktiv

ENGLISH-GERMAN

audience das Publikum
August der August
aunt die Tante
Australia Australien
Australian australisch;
 (man) der Australier;
 (woman) die Australierin
Austria Österreich
Austrian österreichisch
automatic automatisch
autumn der Herbst
awake wach
awful furchtbar
axe das Beil
axle die Achse

baby das Baby
baby-sitter der Babysitter
bachelor der Junggeselle
back (of body) der Rücken;
 come back/go back
 zurückkommen/
 zurückgehen; at the back
 hinten; the back wheel/
 seat das Hinterrad/der
 Rücksitz
backpack der Rucksack
bacon der Speck
bad schlecht
badly schlecht
bag die Tasche; (suitcase)
 der Koffer
bake backen
baker's die Bäckerei
balcony der Balkon
bald kahl
ball der Ball
Baltic die Ostsee
banana die Banane

bandage der Verband
bank die Bank
bar die Bar
barbecue das Barbecue
barber der Friseur
barmaid die Bardame
barman der Barkeeper
basement das Souterrain
basket der Korb
bath das Bad
bathing cap die Badekappe
bathroom das Badezimmer
bath salts das Badesalz
bathtub die Badewanne
battery die Batterie
Bavaria Bayern
be sein (see grammar)
beach der Strand
beans die Bohnen fpl; green
 beans grüne Bohnen
beard der Bart
beautiful schön
because weil
become werden
bed das Bett; single/double
 bed das Einzelbett/das
 Doppelbett; go to bed zu
 Bett gehen
bed linen die Bettwäsche
bedroom das Schlafzimmer
bee die Biene
beef das Rindfleisch
beer das Bier
beer mug der Bierkrug
before vor
begin anfangen
beginner der Anfänger
beginning der Anfang
behind hinter
beige beige
Belgian belgisch; (man) der
 Belgier; (woman) die
 Belgierin

Belgium Belgien
believe glauben
bell die Glocke; *(for door, at
  reception etc)* die Klingel
belong gehören
below unter
belt der Gürtel
bend die Kurve
best: the best der/die/das
  beste
better besser
between zwischen
bicycle das Fahrrad
big groß
bikini der Bikini
bill die Rechnung
binding *(ski)* die Bindung
bird der Vogel
biro *(R)* der Kugelschreiber
birthday der Geburtstag;
  happy birthday! viel Glück
  zum Geburtstag!
biscuit das Plätzchen
bit: a little bit ein bißchen
bite der Bissen; *(insect)* der
  Stich
bitter bitter
black schwarz
black and white schwarz-
  weiß
blackberry die Brombeere
bladder die Blase
blanket die Decke
bleach *(for toilets etc)* das
  Reinigungsmittel
bleed bluten
bless: bless you! Gesundheit!
blind blind
blister die Blase
blocked blockiert
blond blond
blood das Blut
blood group die Blutgruppe

blouse die Bluse
blow-dry: to have a blow-dry
  sich fönen lassen
blue blau
boarding pass die Bordkarte
boat das Schiff
body der Körper
boil kochen
bolt der Riegel
bolt *(verb)* verriegeln
bomb die Bombe
bone der Knochen; *(in fish)*
  die Gräte
bonnet *(car)* die Motorhaube
book das Buch
book *(verb)* buchen
bookshop die Buchhandlung
boot *(shoe)* der Stiefel; *(car)*
  der Kofferraum
border die Grenze
boring langweilig
born: I was born in 1963 ich
  bin 1963 geboren
borrow leihen
boss der Chef
both: both of them beide
bottle die Flasche
bottle-opener der
  Flaschenöffner
bottom der Boden; *(of body)*
  der Hintern; **at the bottom
  of the hill** unten am Berg
bowl die Schüssel
box die Schachtel; *(larger)*
  der Karton
box office die Kasse
boy der Junge
boyfriend der Freund
bra der BH
bracelet das Armband
brake die Bremse
brake *(verb)* bremsen
brandy der Weinbrand

ENGLISH-GERMAN

brave mutig
bread das Brot; **white/
  wholemeal bread** das
  Weißbrot/das Vollkornbrot
break zerbrechen
break down eine Panne
  haben
breakdown (*car*) die Panne;
  (*nervous*) der
  Nervenzusammenbruch
breakfast das Frühstück
breast die Brust
breastfeed stillen
breathe atmen
brick der Backstein
bridge (*over river etc*) die
  Brücke
briefcase die Aktentasche
bring bringen
Britain Großbritannien
British britisch
brochure die Broschüre
broke: I'm broke ich bin
  pleite
broken kaputt
brooch die Brosche
broom der Besen
brother der Bruder
brother-in-law der Schwager
brown braun
bruise der blaue Fleck
brush die Bürste
Brussels sprouts der
  Rosenkohl
bucket der Eimer
building das Gebäude
bulb (*light*) die Glühbirne
bumper die Stoßstange
bunk beds das Etagenbett
buoy die Boje
burn die Verbrennung
burn (*verb*) brennen
bus der Bus

business das Geschäft
business trip die
  Geschäftsreise
bus station der Busbahnhof
bus stop die Bushaltestelle
busy (*person*) beschäftigt;
  (*streets*) belebt; (*telephone*)
  besetzt
but aber
butcher's die Metzgerei
butter die Butter
butterfly der Schmetterling
button der Knopf
buy kaufen
by von; **by car** mit dem
  Auto

cabbage der Kohl
cabin (*ship*) die Kabine
cable car die Drahtseilbahn
café das Café
cagoule der Anorak
cake der Kuchen
cake shop die Konditorei
calculator der
  Taschenrechner
calendar der Kalender
call rufen; (*phone*) anrufen
calm down sich beruhigen
Calor gas (*R*) das Butangas
camera die Kamera
campbed die Campingliege
camping das Camping
campsite der Campingplatz
can die Dose
can: I/she can ich/sie kann;
  can you ...? können
  Sie ...?

ENGLISH-GERMAN

Canada Kanada
Canadian kanadisch; (man) der Kanadier; (woman) die Kanadierin
canal der Kanal
cancel streichen
candle die Kerze
canoe das Kanu
cap (hat) die Mütze
captain der Kapitän
car das Auto
caravan der Wohnwagen
caravan site der Campingplatz
carburettor der Vergaser
card die Karte; (business) die Visitenkarte
cardboard die Pappe
cardigan die Wolljacke
car driver der Autofahrer
care: take care of aufpassen auf (+acc)
careful vorsichtig
car park der Parkplatz
carpet der Teppich
car rental die Autovermietung
carriage der Wagen
carrot die Mohrrübe
carry tragen
carry-cot die Säuglingstragetasche
cash: pay cash bar zahlen
cash desk die Kasse
cash dispenser der Geldautomat
cassette die Kassette
cassette player der Kassettenrecorder
castle das Schloß
cat die Katze
catch fangen; which bus do I catch? welchen Bus muß

ich nehmen?
cathedral der Dom
Catholic katholisch
cauliflower der Blumenkohl
cause der Grund
cave die Höhle
ceiling die Decke
cemetery der Friedhof
centigrade Celsius
central heating die Zentralheizung
centre das Zentrum
century das Jahrhundert
certificate die Bescheinigung
chain die Kette
chair der Stuhl
chairlift der Sessellift
chalet das Chalet
chambermaid das Zimmermädchen
chance: by chance durch Zufall
change (small) das Kleingeld
change (verb) wechseln; (clothes) sich umziehen; change trains umsteigen
changeable (weather) wechselhaft
Channel der Kanal
charter flight der Charterflug
cheap billig
check (verb) prüfen
check-in die Abfertigung
cheers! prost!
cheese der Käse
chemist's die Apotheke
cheque der Scheck
cheque book das Scheckheft
cheque card die Scheckkarte
cherry die Kirsche
chest die Brust
chestnut die Kastanie
chewing gum der Kaugummi

chicken das Huhn; (*food*) das Hähnchen
child das Kind
children's portion der Kinderteller
chin das Kinn
chips die Pommes frites *pl*
chocolate die Schokolade; **milk chocolate** die Vollmilchschokolade; **plain chocolate** die Bitterschokolade; **hot chocolate** der Kakao
choke (*on car*) der Choke
choose wählen
chop (*meat*) das Kotelett
Christian name der Vorname
Christmas Weihnachten
church die Kirche
cider der Cidre
cigar die Zigarre
cigarette die Zigarette
cinema das Kino
city die Stadt
city centre die Stadtmitte
class die Klasse; **first class** die erste Klasse; **second class** die zweite Klasse
classical music die klassische Musik
clean (*adjective*) sauber
clean (*verb*) reinigen
cleansing cream die Reinigungscreme
clear klar
clever klug
cliff die Klippe
climate das Klima
cloakroom (*coats*) die Garderobe
clock die Uhr
close (*verb*) schließen
closed geschlossen

clothes die Kleider *pl*
clothes peg die Wäscheklammer
cloud die Wolke
cloudy bewölkt
club der Klub
clutch die Kupplung
coach der Bus; (*of train*) der Wagen
coast die Küste
coat der Mantel
coathanger der Kleiderbügel
cockroach die Küchenschabe
cocktail der Cocktail
cocoa der Kakao
coffee der Kaffee; **white coffee** Kaffee mit Milch
cold kalt; **I'm cold** mir ist kalt
cold (*illness*) die Erkältung; **I've got a cold** ich bin erkältet
cold cream die Feuchtigkeitscreme
collar der Kragen
collection die Sammlung
colour die Farbe
colour film der Farbfilm
comb der Kamm
come kommen; **come in!** herein!
comfortable bequem
compact disc die Compact-Disc
company die Firma
compartment das Abteil
compass der Kompaß
complain sich beschweren
complicated kompliziert
compliment das Kompliment
computer der Computer
concert das Konzert
conditioner der Haarfestiger

condom das Kondom
conductor (*bus*) der Schaffner
confirm bestätigen
congratulations! herzlichen
Glückwunsch!
connection die Verbindung
constipated verstopft
consulate das Konsulat
contact (*get in touch with*)
erreichen
contact lenses die
Kontaktlinsen *fpl*
contraceptive das
Verhütungsmittel
cook der Koch
cook (*verb*) kochen
cooker der Herd
cooking utensils das
Kochgeschirr
cool kühl
corkscrew der Korkenzieher
corner die Ecke
correct richtig
corridor der Flur
cosmetics die Kosmetika *npl*
cost kosten
cot das Kinderbett
cotton die Baumwolle
cotton wool die Watte
couchette der Liegewagen
cough der Husten
cough (*verb*) husten
country das Land
countryside die Landschaft;
in the countryside auf dem
Land
course: of course natürlich
cousin (*male*) der Vetter;
(*female*) die Kusine
cow die Kuh
crab die Krabbe
crafts das Handwerk
cramp der Krampf

crankshaft die Kurbelwelle
crash der Zusammenstoß
cream (*food*) die Sahne; (*for
skin etc*) die Creme
cream puff der Windbeutel
credit card die Kreditkarte
crew die Mannschaft
crisps die Chips *pl*
crockery das Geschirr
cross (*verb*) überqueren
crowd die Menge
crowded voll
cruise die Kreuzfahrt
crutches die Krücken *fpl*
cry weinen
cuckoo clock die
Kuckucksuhr
cucumber die Gurke
cup die Tasse
cupboard der Schrank
curry der Curry
curtain der Vorhang
custom der Brauch
customs der Zoll
cut (*verb*) schneiden
cutlery das Besteck
cycling das Radfahren
cyclist der Radfahrer
cylinder head gasket die
Zylinderkopfdichtung

dad der Vati
damage (*verb*) beschädigen
damp feucht
dance (*verb*) tanzen
danger die Gefahr
dangerous gefährlich
dare wagen
dark dunkel

ENGLISH-GERMAN

dashboard das Armaturenbrett
date (*time*) das Datum
daughter die Tochter
daughter-in-law die Schwiegertochter
day der Tag
dead tot
deaf taub
dear teuer
death der Tod
decaffeinated koffeinfrei
December der Dezember
decide entscheiden
deck das Deck
deck chair der Liegestuhl
deep tief
delay die Verzögerung
deliberately absichtlich
delicious köstlich
demand fordern
dentist der Zahnarzt
dentures das Gebiß
deodorant das Deodorant
department store das Kaufhaus
departure die Abfahrt
depend: it depends das kommt darauf an
depressed deprimiert
dessert der Nachtisch
develop entwickeln
device das Gerät
diabetic: I'm diabetic ich bin Diabetiker(in)
dialect der Dialekt
dialling code die Vorwahl
diamond der Diamant
diarrhoea der Durchfall
diary das Tagebuch
dictionary das Wörterbuch
die sterben
diesel (*fuel*) der Diesel

diet die Diät
different verschieden
difficult schwierig
dining car der Speisewagen
dining room das Eßzimmer; (*in hotel*) das Speisezimmer
dinner das Abendessen; **have dinner** zu Abend essen
direct direkt
direction die Richtung
directory enquiries die Auskunft
dirty schmutzig
disabled behindert
disappear verschwinden
disappointed enttäuscht
disaster die Katastrophe
disco die Diskothek
disease die Krankheit
disgusting widerlich
disinfectant das Desinfektionsmittel
distance der Abstand
distributor der Verteiler
district (*in town*) das Viertel
disturb stören
dive tauchen
divorced geschieden
do tun; **that'll do nicely** prima
doctor der Arzt
document das Dokument; **documents please** Papiere bitte
dog der Hund
doll die Puppe
door die Tür
double doppelt
double room das Doppelzimmer
down: down there dort unten

downstairs unten
draught der Zug
dream der Traum
dress das Kleid
dress (*someone*) anziehen;
(*oneself*) sich anziehen
dressing gown der
Bademantel
drink das Getränk;
(*alcoholic*) der Drink
drink (*verb*) trinken
drinking water das
Trinkwasser
drive fahren
driver der Fahrer
driving licence der
Führerschein
drop der Tropfen
drop (*verb*) fallenlassen
drug (*narcotic*) die Droge
drunk betrunken
dry trocken
dry (*verb*) trocknen
dry-cleaner die chemische
Reinigung
duck die Ente
durex (*R*) das Präservativ
during während
dustbin die Mülltonne
Dutch holländisch
duty-free zollfrei
duty-free shop der Duty-
free-Laden

each jeder, jede, jedes; **how
much are they each?** was
kosten sie das Stück?
ear das Ohr

early früh; (*too early*) zu früh
earrings die Ohrringe *mpl*
earth die Erde
east der Osten; **east of**
östlich von
Easter Ostern
easy leicht
eat essen
egg das Ei; **boiled egg** das
gekochte Ei; **hard-boiled
egg** das hartgekochte Ei
egg cup der Eierbecher
either ... or ... entweder ...
oder ...
elastic elastisch
Elastoplast (*R*) das
Hansaplast (*R*)
elbow der Ellbogen
electric elektrisch
electricity die Elektrizität
else: something else etwas
anderes
elsewhere woanders
embarrassing peinlich
embassy die Botschaft
emergency der Notfall
emergency exit der
Notausgang
empty leer
end das Ende
engaged (*toilet, phone*)
besetzt; (*to be married*)
verlobt
engine der Motor; (*train*) die
Lokomotive
England England
English englisch; **the
English** die Engländer
English girl/woman die
Engländerin
Englishman der Engländer
enlargement die
Vergrößerung

ENGLISH-GERMAN

enough genug; **that's enough** das reicht
enter eintreten in (+*acc*)
entrance der Eingang
envelope der Umschlag
epileptic: he's epileptic er ist Epileptiker
especially besonders
Eurocheque der Euroscheck
Europe Europa
European europäisch
even: even men/if selbst Männer/wenn; **even more beautiful** noch schöner
evening der Abend; **good evening** guten Abend
every jeder, jede, jedes; **every time** jedesmal; **every day** jeden Tag
everyone jeder
everything alles
everywhere überall
exaggerate übertreiben
example das Beispiel; **for example** zum Beispiel
excellent ausgezeichnet
except außer
excess baggage das Übergewicht
exchange tauschen
exchange rate der Wechselkurs
exciting aufregend
excuse me Entschuldigung!
exhaust der Auspuff
exhibition die Ausstellung
exit der Ausgang
expensive teuer
explain erklären
extension lead die Verlängerungsschnur
eye das Auge
eyebrow die Augenbraue

eyeliner der Eyeliner
eye shadow der Lidschatten

face das Gesicht
factory die Fabrik
faint (*verb*) in Ohnmacht fallen
fair (*funfair*) der Jahrmarkt; (*trade*) die Messe
fair (*adjective*) gerecht
fall fallen
false falsch
family die Familie
famous berühmt
fan der Ventilator
fan belt der Keilriemen
far (away) weit
farm der Bauernhof
farmer der Bauer
fashion die Mode
fashionable modisch
fast schnell
fat das Fett
fat (*adjective*) dick
father der Vater
father-in-law der Schwiegervater
fault der Fehler; **it's my/his fault** ich bin/er ist schuld
faulty fehlerhaft
favourite (*adjective*) Lieblings-
fear die Angst
February der Februar
fed up: I'm fed up (with) ich habe genug (von)
feel fühlen; **I feel well/ unwell** ich fühle mich gut/ schlecht; **I feel like** ich habe Lust auf (+*acc*)

65

ENGLISH-GERMAN

feeling das Gefühl
felt-tip pen der Filzstift
feminist feministisch
fence der Zaun
ferry die Fähre
fever das Fieber
few: few tourists wenig
  Touristen; **a few** einige
fiancé(e) der Verlobte, die
  Verlobte
field das Feld
fight der Kampf
fight (*verb*) kämpfen
fill füllen
fillet das Filet
filling (*tooth*) die Plombe
film der Film
filter der Filter
find finden
fine die Geldstrafe
fine (*weather*) schön
finger der Finger
fingernail der Fingernagel
finish beenden
fire das Feuer
fire brigade die Feuerwehr
fire extinguisher der
  Feuerlöscher
fireworks das Feuerwerk
first erster, erste, erstes;
  (*firstly*) zunächst
first aid die Erste Hilfe
first class erster Klasse
first floor der erste Stock
first name der Vorname
fish der Fisch
fishbone die Gräte
fishing das Angeln
fishmonger's das
  Fischgeschaft
fit (*healthy*) fit
fizzy mit Kohlensäure
flag die Fahne

flash der Blitz
flat die Wohnung
flat (*adjective*) flach; (*tyre*)
  platt
flavour der Geschmack
flea der Floh
flight der Flug
flirt flirten
floor der Boden; (*storey*) der
  Stock
florist die Blumenhandlung
flour das Mehl
flower die Blume
flu die Grippe
fly die Fliege
fly (*verb*) fliegen
fog der Nebel
folk music der Folk
follow folgen (+*dat*)
food das Essen
food poisoning die
  Lebensmittelvergiftung
foot der Fuß; **on foot** zu Fuß
football der Fußball
for für
forbidden verboten
forehead die Stirn
foreign ausländisch
foreigner der Ausländer
forest der Wald
forget vergessen
fork die Gabel; (*in road*) die
  Abzweigung
form das Formular
fortnight: a fortnight
  vierzehn Tage
fortunately zum Glück
forward (*mail*) nachsenden
foundation cream die
  Grundierungscreme
fountain der Brunnen
fracture der Bruch
France Frankreich

ENGLISH-GERMAN

free frei; (*of charge*) gratis
freezer die Gefriertruhe
French französisch
fresh frisch
Friday der Freitag
fridge der Kühlschrank
friend der Freund, die Freundin
from: from Cologne to Munich von Köln nach München
front (*part*) die Vorderseite; **in front of** vor
frost der Frost
frozen food die Tiefkühlkost
fruit das Obst
fry braten
frying pan die Bratpfanne
full voll
full board die Vollpension
fun: have fun sich amüsieren; **have fun!** viel Spaß!
funeral die Beerdigung
funnel (*for pouring*) der Trichter
funny (*strange, amusing*) komisch
furious wütend
furniture die Möbel *pl*
further weiter
fuse die Sicherung
future die Zukunft

G

game (*to play*) das Spiel; (*meat*) das Wild
garage die Garage; (*repairs*) die Werkstatt; (*petrol*) die Tankstelle

garden der Garten
garlic der Knoblauch
gas das Gas
gas permeable lenses die luftdurchlässigen Kontaktlinsen *fpl*
gay homosexuell
gear der Gang
gearbox das Getriebe
gear lever der Schaltknüppel
gentleman der Herr
gents (*toilet*) die Herrentoilette
genuine echt
German deutsch
German (*man/woman*) der Deutsche, die Deutsche
Germany Deutschland
get bekommen; **can you tell me how to get to . . .?** können Sie mir sagen, wie ich zum/zur . . . komme?; **get back** (*return*) zurückkehren; **get in** (*car*) einsteigen; **get off** aussteigen; **get up** aufstehen; **get out!** raus!
gin der Gin
girl das Mädchen
girlfriend die Freundin
give geben; **give back** zurückgeben
glad froh
glass das Glas
glasses die Brille
gloves die Handschuhe *mpl*
glue der Leim
go gehen; **go in** hineingehen; **go out** hinausgehen; **go down** hinuntergehen; **go up** hinaufgehen; **go through** hindurchgehen; **go away**

weggehen; **go away!**
verschwinden Sie!
goat die Ziege
God Gott
gold das Gold
golf das Golf
good gut
goodbye auf Wiedersehen
goose die Gans
got: have you got . . . ? haben
Sie . . . ?
government die Regierung
grammar die Grammatik
grandfather der Großvater
grandmother die Großmutter
grapefruit die Pampelmuse
grapes die Trauben *fpl*
grass das Gras
grateful dankbar
greasy fett
Greece Griechenland
Greek griechisch
green grün
greengrocer der
Gemüsehändler
grey grau
grilled gegrillt
grocer's die
Lebensmittelhandlung
ground floor das Erdgeschoß
group die Gruppe
guarantee die Garantie
guest der Gast
guesthouse die Pension
guide der Reiseführer
guidebook der Reiseführer
guitar die Gitarre
gun *(rifle)* das Gewehr;
(pistol) die Pistole

habit die Gewohnheit
hail *(ice)* der Hagel
hair das Haar
haircut der Haarschnitt
hairdresser der Friseur
hair dryer der Fön *(R)*
hair spray das Haarspray
half die Hälfte; **half a litre/
day** einen halben Liter/
Tag; **half an hour** eine
halbe Stunde
half board die Halbpension
ham der Schinken
hamburger der Hamburger
hammer der Hammer
hand die Hand
handbag die Handtasche
handbrake die Handbremse
handkerchief das
Taschentuch
handle der Griff
hand luggage das
Handgepäck
handsome gutaussehend
hanger der Kleiderbügel
hangover der Kater
happen geschehen
happy glücklich; **happy
Christmas/New Year!** frohe
Weihnachten/frohes neues
Jahr
harbour der Hafen
hard hart
hard lenses die harten
Kontaktlinsen *fpl*
hat der Hut
hate hassen
have haben *(see grammar)*; **I
have to . . .** ich muß . . .

hay fever das Heufieber
hazelnut die Haselnuß
he er
head der Kopf
headache das Kopfweh
headlights die Scheinwerfer *mpl*
health die Gesundheit
healthy gesund
hear hören
hearing aid das Hörgerät
heart das Herz
heart attack der Herzinfarkt
heat die Wärme
heater das Heizgerät
heating die Heizung
heavy schwer
heel die Ferse; (*of shoe*) der Absatz
helicopter der Hubschrauber
hello guten Tag
help die Hilfe
help (*verb*) helfen
her (*possessive*) ihr, ihre, ihr; (*object*) sie, ihr (*see grammar*)
herbs die Kräuter *npl*
here hier; **come here!** kommen Sie her!
hers: it's hers es gehört ihr (*see grammar*)
hiccups der Schluckauf
hide verbergen
high hoch
highway code die Straßenverkehrsordnung
hill der Berg
him ihn, ihm (*see grammar*)
hip die Hüfte
hire: for hire zu vermieten
his sein, seine, sein; **it's his** es gehört ihm (*see grammar*)
history die Geschichte
hit schlagen

hitchhike trampen
hitchhiking das Trampen
hobby das Hobby
hold halten
hole das Loch
holiday der Urlaub; (*public*) der Feiertag; **summer holidays** die Sommerferien *pl*
Holland Holland
home: at home zu Hause; **go home** nach Hause gehen
homemade hausgemacht
homesick: I'm homesick ich habe Heimweh
honest ehrlich
honey der Honig
honeymoon die Flitterwochen *pl*
hoover (*R*) der Staubsauger
hope hoffen
horn (*of car*) die Hupe
horrible furchtbar
horse das Pferd
horse riding der Reitsport
hospital das Krankenhaus
hospitality die Gastfreundschaft
hot heiß; (*to taste*) scharf
hotel das Hotel
hot-water bottle die Wärmflasche
hour die Stunde
house das Haus
house wine der Tafelwein
how? wie?; **how are you?** wie geht es Ihnen?; **how are things?** wie geht's?; **how many?** wie viele; **how much?** wieviel?
humour der Humor
hungry: I'm hungry ich habe Hunger

hurry (*verb*) sich beeilen;
hurry up! beeilen Sie sich!
hurt verletzen; it hurts es
tut weh
husband der Mann

I ich
ice das Eis
ice cream das Eis
ice lolly das Eis am Stiel
idea die Idee
idiot der Idiot
if falls
ignition die Zündung
ill krank
immediately sofort
important wichtig
impossible unmöglich
improve verbessern
in in; in London in
London; in 1945 1945; in
English auf englisch; is he
in? ist er da?
included inbegriffen
incredible unglaublich
independent unabhängig
indicator (*car*) der Blinker
indigestion die
Magenverstimmung
industry die Industrie
infection die Entzündung
information die Information
information desk die
Auskunft
injection die Spritze
injured verletzt
inner tube der Schlauch
innocent unschuldig

insect das Insekt
insect repellent das
Insektenschutzmittel
inside (*in building, box etc*)
drinnen
insomnia die Schlaflosigkeit
instant coffee der
Pulverkaffee
instructor der Lehrer
insurance die Versicherung
intelligent intelligent
interesting interessant
introduce vorstellen
invitation die Einladung
invite einladen
Ireland Irland
Irish irisch
iron (*metal*) das Eisen; (*for
clothes*) das Bügeleisen
iron (*verb*) bügeln
ironmonger's die
Eisenwarenhandlung
island die Insel
it es
Italian italienisch
Italy Italien
itch das Jucken
IUD die Spirale

jack (*car*) der Wagenheber
jacket die Jacke
jam die Marmelade
January der Januar
jaw der Kiefer
jazz der Jazz
jealous eifersüchtig
jeans die Jeans
jellyfish die Qualle

ENGLISH-GERMAN

jeweller's der Juwelier
jewellery der Schmuck
Jewish jüdisch
job die Arbeit
jogging das Jogging; **go jogging** joggen gehen
joint (*to smoke*) der Joint
joke der Witz
journey die Reise
jug der Krug
juice der Saft
July der Juli
jump springen
jumper der Pullover
junction die Kreuzung
June der Juni
just: just two nur zwei

keep behalten
kettle der Wasserkessel
key der Schlüssel
kidneys die Nieren *fpl*
kill töten
kilo das Kilo
kilometre der Kilometer
kind freundlich
king der König
kiss der Kuß
kiss (*verb*) küssen
kitchen die Küche
knee das Knie
knife das Messer
knit stricken
knock over umstoßen; (*car*) anfahren
know wissen; (*person, place*) kennen; **I don't know** ich weiß nicht

label das Etikett
ladder die Leiter
ladies (*toilet*) die Damentoilette
lady die Dame
lager das helle Bier
lake der See
lamb das Lamm
lamp die Lampe
land (*verb*) landen
landscape die Landschaft
language die Sprache
language school die Sprachenschule
large groß
last letzte; **last year** letztes Jahr; **at last** endlich
late spät; **be/arrive late** zu spät kommen/ankommen
laugh lachen
launderette der Waschsalon
laundry (*to wash*) die Wäsche; (*place*) die Wäscherei
law das Gesetz
lawn der Rasen
lawyer der Rechtsanwalt
laxative das Abführmittel
lazy faul
leaf das Blatt
leaflet der Handzettel
leak das Leck
learn lernen
least: at least mindestens
leather das Leder
leave lassen; (*go away*) abreisen; (*forget*) vergessen
left links; **on the left (of)** links (von)

ENGLISH-GERMAN

left-handed linkshändig
left luggage die
  Gepäckaufbewahrung
leg das Bein
lemon die Zitrone
lemonade die Limonade
lemon tea der Zitronentee
lend leihen
length die Länge
lens die Linse
less weniger
lesson die Stunde
let (*allow*) lassen
letter der Brief
letterbox der Briefkasten
lettuce der Salat
level crossing der
  Bahnübergang
library die Bücherei
licence die Genehmigung
lid der Deckel
lie (*say untruth*) lügen
lie down sich hinlegen
life das Leben
lift (*elevator*) der Fahrstuhl;
  give a lift to mitnehmen
light das Licht; **have you got
  a light?** haben Sie Feuer?
light (*adjective*) leicht; **light
  blue** hellblau
light (*verb*) anzünden
light bulb die Glühbirne
lighter das Feuerzeug
lighthouse der Leuchtturm
light meter der
  Belichtungsmesser
like mögen; **I would like
  . . .** ich möchte gern . . .
like (*as*) wie
lip die Lippe
lipstick der Lippenstift
liqueur der Likör
list die Liste

lip die Lippe
lipstick der Lippenstift
liqueur der Likör
list die Liste
listen (to) zuhören (+*dat*)
litre der Liter
litter der Abfall
little wenig; **a little bit (of)**
  ein bißchen
live leben; (*in town etc*)
  wohnen
liver die Leber
living room das
  Wohnzimmer
lobster der Hummer
lock das Schloß
lock (*verb*) abschließen
lollipop der Lutscher
long lang
look: look (at) ansehen;
  (*seem*) scheinen; **look like**
  ähneln (+*dat*); **look for**
  suchen; **look out!**
  Achtung!
lorry der Lastwagen
lose verlieren
lost property office das
  Fundbüro
lot: a lot (of) viel
loud laut
lounge der Salon
love die Liebe; **make love to**
  schlafen mit
love (*verb*) lieben
lovely herrlich
low tief
luck das Glück; **good luck!**
  viel Glück!
luggage das Gepäck
lukewarm lauwarm
lunch das Mittagessen
lungs die Lunge

macho macho
mad verrückt
magazine das Magazin
maiden name der
    Mädchenname
mail die Post
main Haupt-
make machen
make-up das Make-up
male chauvinist pig der
    Chauvi
man der Mann
manager der Geschäftsführer
many viele
map die Landkarte; (of
    town) der Stadtplan
March der März
margarine die Margarine
market der Markt
marmalade die
    Orangenmarmelade
married verheiratet
mascara die Wimperntusche
mass der Gottesdienst
match (light) das Streichholz;
    (sport) das Spiel
material der Stoff
matter: it doesn't matter das
    macht nichts
mattress die Matratze
May der Mai
maybe vielleicht
mayonnaise die Mayonnaise
me mich, mir; for me für
    mich; me too ich auch; it's
    me ich bin's (see grammar)
meal die Mahlzeit; enjoy
    your meal! guten Appetit!

mean (verb) bedeuten
measles die Masern pl;
    German measles die
    Röteln pl
meat das Fleisch
mechanic der Mechaniker
medicine die Medizin
Mediterranean das
    Mittelmeer
medium (steak) medium
medium-sized mittelgroß
meet treffen
meeting das Treffen
melon die Melone
mend reparieren
menu die Speisekarte; set
    menu die Tageskarte
mess das Durcheinander
message die Nachricht
metal das Metall
metre der Meter
midday der Mittag
middle die Mitte
Middle Ages das Mittelalter
midnight die Mitternacht
milk die Milch
minced meat das Hackfleisch
mind: do you mind if I ...?
    stört es Sie, wenn ich ...
mine: it's mine es gehört mir
    (see grammar)
mineral water das
    Mineralwasser
minute die Minute
mirror der Spiegel
Miss Fräulein, Frl.
miss vermissen; (train etc)
    verpassen
mistake der Fehler
misunderstanding das
    Mißverständnis
mix mischen
modern modern

moisturizer die Feuchtigkeitscreme
Monday der Montag
money das Geld
month der Monat
monument das Denkmal
mood die Stimmung
moon der Mond
moped das Moped
more mehr; **no more . . .** keine . . . mehr
morning der Morgen; **good morning** guten Morgen
mosquito die Stechmücke
most (of) das meiste (von); **most people** die meisten Leute
mother die Mutter
motorbike das Motorrad
motorboat das Motorboot
motorway die Autobahn
mountain der Berg
mouse die Maus
moustache der Schnurrbart
mouth der Mund
move (*change position*) sich bewegen
Mr Herr
Mrs Frau
Ms Frau
much viel
mum die Mutti
muscle der Muskel
museum das Museum
mushrooms die Pilze *mpl*
music die Musik
musical instrument das Musikinstrument
mussels die Muscheln *fpl*
must: I/you must ich muß/Sie müssen; **you must not** Sie dürfen nicht
mustard der Senf

my mein, meine, mein (*see grammar*)

nail der Nagel
nail clippers die Nagelschere
nailfile die Nagelfeile
nail polish der Nagellack
nail polish remover der Nagellackentferner
naked nackt
name der Name; **what's your name?** wie heißen Sie?; **my name is Jim** ich heiße Jim
napkin die Serviette
nappy die Windel
nappy-liners die Windeleinlagen *fpl*
narrow eng
nationality die Staatsangehörigkeit
natural natürlich
nature die Natur
near nah(e) (*+dat*); **near here** in der Nähe; **the nearest . . .** der/die/das nächste . . .
nearly fast
necessary notwendig
neck der Hals
necklace die Halskette
need brauchen
needle die Nadel
negative (*film*) das Negativ
neighbour der Nachbar, die Nachbarin
neither . . . nor . . . weder . . . noch

nephew der Neffe
nervous nervös
neurotic neurotisch
never nie
new neu
news die Nachrichten *fpl*
newsagent der Zeitungshändler
newspaper die Zeitung
New Year das Neujahr
next nächste; **next year** nächstes Jahr
next to neben (+*dat*)
nice nett; (*food*) gut
nickname der Spitzname
niece die Nichte
night die Nacht; **good night** gute Nacht!
nightclub der Nachtklub
nightdress das Nachthemd
nightmare der Alptraum
no nein; **no ... kein ...**
nobody niemand
noise der Lärm
noisy laut
non-smoking Nichtraucher
normal normal
north der Norden; **north of** nördlich von
Northern Ireland Nordirland
nose die Nase
not nicht
note (*money*) der Geldschein
notebook das Notizbuch
nothing nichts
novel der Roman
November der November
now jetzt
nowhere nirgends
number (*house, phone*) die Nummer
number plate das Nummernschild
nurse die Krankenschwester; (*male*) der Krankenpfleger
nut (*to eat*) die Nuß; (*for bolt*) die Mutter

obnoxious widerwärtig
obvious offensichtlich
October der Oktober
of von (*see grammar*)
off (*lights*) aus
offer anbieten
office das Büro
often oft
oil das Öl
ointment die Salbe
OK okay; **I'm OK** mir geht's gut
old alt; **how old are you?** wie alt sind Sie?; **I'm 25 years old** ich bin 25 Jahre (alt)
old-age pensioner der Rentner, die Rentnerin
olive die Olive
omelette das Omelette
on auf; (*lights*) an
once einmal
one ein, *f* eine
onion die Zwiebel
only nur
open (*adjective*) offen
open (*verb*) öffnen
opera die Oper
operation die Operation
opposite das Gegenteil

ENGLISH-GERMAN

opposite: opposite the
  church gegenüber der
  Kirche
optician der Augenarzt
optimistic optimistisch
or oder
orange die Orange
orange (*colour*) orange
orchestra das Orchester
order befehlen
organize organisieren
other andere
otherwise sonst
our unser, uns(e)re, unser
  (*see grammar*)
out aus; **he's out** er ist nicht
  da
outside außen
oven der Backofen
over (*above*) über; (*finished*)
  vorbei; **over there** dort
  drüben
overdone verkocht
overtake überholen
owner der Besitzer
oyster die Auster

pack (*verb*) packen
package das Paket
package tour die
  Pauschalreise
packed lunch das
  Lunchpaket
packet (*of cigarettes etc*) die
  Schachtel
page die Seite
pain der Schmerz
painful schmerzhaft

painkiller das Schmerzmittel
paint (*verb*) streichen
paint brush (*artist's*) der
  Pinsel
painting das Gemälde
pair das Paar; **a pair of**
  shoes ein Paar Schuhe
palace der Palast
pancake der Pfannkuchen
panic die Panik
panties das Höschen
paper das Papier
parcel das Paket
pardon? bitte?
parents die Eltern *pl*
park der Park
park (*verb*) parken
party (*celebration*) die Fete;
  (*group*) die Gruppe
pass (*mountain*) der Paß
passenger der Passagier
passport der Paß
pasta die Nudeln *fpl*
pâté die Pastete
path der Weg
pavement der Bürgersteig
pay zahlen
peach der Pfirsich
peanuts die Erdnüsse *fpl*
pear die Birne
peas die Erbsen *fpl*
pedal das Pedal
pedestrian der Fußgänger
pedestrian crossing der
  Fußgängerüberweg
pedestrian precinct die
  Fußgängerzone
pen der Stift
pencil der Bleistift
pencil sharpener der Spitzer
penicillin das Penizillin
penis der Penis
penknife das Taschenmesser

ENGLISH-GERMAN

people die Leute *pl*
pepper (*spice*) der Pfeffer;
  (*vegetable*) die
  Paprikaschote
per: per week pro Woche;
  per cent Prozent
perfect perfekt
perfume das Parfüm
period die Periode
perm die Dauerwelle
person die Person
petrol das Benzin
petrol station die Tankstelle
phone (*verb*) anrufen
phone book das Telefonbuch
phone box die Telefonzelle
phone number die
  Telefonnummer
photograph das Foto
photograph (*verb*)
  fotografieren
photographer der Fotograf
phrase book der
  Sprachführer
pickpocket der Taschendieb
picnic das Picknick
pie (*fruit*) der Kuchen;
  (*meat*) die Pastete
piece das Stück
pig das Schwein
piles die Hämorrhoiden *pl*
pill die Pille
pillow das Kopfkissen
pilot der Pilot
pin die Nadel
pineapple die Ananas
pink rosa
pipe das Rohr; (*to smoke*) die
  Pfeife
pity: it's a pity das ist schade
pizza die Pizza
plane das Flugzeug
plant die Pflanze

plastic das Plastik
plastic bag die Plastiktüte
plate der Teller
platform (*station*) der
  Bahnsteig
play (*theatre*) das Stück
play (*verb*) spielen
pleasant angenehm
please bitte
pleased zufrieden; **pleased
  to meet you!** freut mich!
pliers die Zange
plug (*electrical*) der Stecker;
  (*in sink*) der Stöpsel
plum die Pflaume
plumber der Klempner
p.m.: 3 p.m. 3 Uhr
  nachmittags, 15 Uhr; **11
  p.m.** 11 Uhr abends, 23 Uhr
pneumonia die
  Lungenentzündung
pocket die Tasche
poison das Gift
police die Polizei
policeman der Polizist
police station die
  Polizeiwache
polite höflich
political politisch
politics die Politik
polluted verschmutzt
pond der Teich
pony das Pony
poor arm
pop music die Popmusik
pork das Schweinefleisch
port (*drink*) der Portwein
porter (*hotel*) der Portier
possible möglich
post (*verb*) aufgeben
postcard die Postkarte
poster (*for room*) das Poster;
  (*in street*) das Plakat

poste restante postlagernd
postman der Briefträger
post office die Post
potato die Kartoffel
poultry das Geflügel
pound das Pfund
power cut der Stromausfall
practical praktisch
pram der Kinderwagen
prawn die Krabbe
prefer vorziehen
pregnant schwanger
prepare vorbereiten
prescription das Rezept
present (*gift*) das Geschenk
pretty hübsch; **pretty good** ganz gut
price der Preis
priest der Geistliche
prince der Prinz
princess die Prinzessin
printed matter die Drucksache
prison das Gefängnis
private privat
probably wahrscheinlich
problem das Problem
programme das Programm
prohibited verboten
promise (*verb*) versprechen
pronounce aussprechen
protect schützen
Protestant evangelisch
proud stolz
public öffentlich
pull ziehen
pump die Pumpe
puncture die Reifenpanne
punk der Punk
purple violett
purse das Portemonnaie
push drücken
pushchair der Sportwagen

put tun; **where can I put my car?** wo kann ich mein Auto hinstellen?
pyjamas der Schlafanzug

quality die Qualität
quarter das Viertel
quay der Kai
queen die Königin
question die Frage
queue die Schlange
queue (*verb*) Schlange stehen
quick(ly) schnell
quiet ruhig; **quiet!** Ruhe!
quilt das Federbett
quite ganz

rabbit das Kaninchen
radiator der Kühler; (*in room*) der Heizkörper
radio das Radio
railway die Eisenbahn
rain der Regen
rain (*verb*) regnen; **it's raining** es regnet
rainbow der Regenbogen
raincoat der Regenmantel
rape die Vergewaltigung
rare selten; (*steak*) englisch
raspberry die Himbeere
rat die Ratte
rather ziemlich; **I'd rather**

... ich würde lieber ...
raw roh
razor der Rasierapparat
razor blade die Rasierklinge
read lesen
ready fertig
really wirklich
rear lights die Rücklichter *npl*
rearview mirror der
  Rückspiegel
receipt die Quittung
receive erhalten
reception (*hotel*) die
  Rezeption
receptionist der
  Empfangschef, die
  Empfangsdame
recipe das Rezept
recognize erkennen
recommend empfehlen
record die Schallplatte
record player der
  Plattenspieler
record shop das
  Schallplattengeschäft
red rot
red-headad rothaarig
refund erstatten
relax sich ausruhen
religion die Religion
remember sich erinnern an
  (*+acc*); **I remember** ich
  erinnere mich daran
rent die Miete
rent (*verb*) mieten
repair reparieren
repeat wiederholen
reservation die Reservierung
reserve reservieren
responsible verantwortlich
rest (*remaining*) der Rest;
  (*sleep*) die Ruhe; **take a**
  rest sich ausruhen

restaurant das Restaurant
return ticket die
  Rückfahrkarte
reverse (*gear*) der
  Rückwärtsgang
rheumatism das Rheuma
rib die Rippe
rice der Reis
rich reich; (*food*) schwer
ridiculous lächerlich
right (*side*) rechts; **on the**
  right (**of**) rechts (von)
right (*correct*) richtig
right of way die Vorfahrt
ring der Ring
ring (*phone*) anrufen
ripe reif
river der Fluß
road die Straße
roadsign das
  Verkehrszeichen
roadworks die
  Straßenbauarbeiten *fpl*
rock der Felsen
rock climbing das
  Felsenklettern
rock music der Rock
roll das Brötchen
roof das Dach
roof rack der
  Dachgepäckträger
room das Zimmer
rope das Seil
rose die Rose
rotten (*lousy*) mies
round (*circular*) rund
roundabout der Kreisverkehr
route die Strecke
rowing boat das Ruderboot
rubber das Gummi; (*eraser*)
  der Radiergummi
rubber band das
  Gummiband

rubbish der Abfall;
  rubbish! Quatsch!; **these
  are rubbish** die sind nichts
rucksack der Rucksack
rude unhöflich
rug der Läufer
ruins die Ruinen *fpl*
rum der Rum
run laufen

sad traurig
safe sicher
safety pin die
  Sicherheitsnadel
sailboard das Windsurfbrett
sailing das Segeln
sailing boat das Segelboot
salad der Salat
salad dressing die Salatsoße
sale der Verkauf; (*reduced
  price*) der Ausverkauf; **for
  sale** zu verkaufen
salmon der Lachs
salt das Salz
salty salzig
same selbe
sand der Sand
sandals die Sandalen *fpl*
sand dunes die Dünen *fpl*
sandwich das belegte Brot
sanitary towel die
  Damenbinde
sardine die Sardine
Saturday der Samstag, der
  Sonnabend
sauce die Soße
saucepan der Kochtopf
saucer die Untertasse

sauna die Sauna
sausage die Wurst
savoury pikant
say sagen
Scandinavia Skandinavien
scarf (*neck*) der Schal; (*head*)
  das Kopftuch
scenery die Landschaft
school die Schule
science die
  Naturwissenschaft
scissors die Schere
Scotland Schottland
Scottish schottisch
scrambled eggs die
  Rührei *npl*
scream schreien
screw die Schraube
screwdriver der
  Schraubenzieher
sea das Meer
seafood die Meeresfrüchte *pl*
seagull die Möwe
seasick seekrank
seaside: at the seaside am
  Meer
season die Jahreszeit; **in the
  high season** in der
  Hauptsaison
seat der Sitz; (*place*) der
  Platz
seat belt der Sicherheitsgurt
seaweed die Algen *fpl*
second zweite; (*in time*) die
  Sekunde
second class zweiter Klasse
second-hand gebraucht
secret geheim
see sehen; **see you
  tomorrow** bis morgen
self-service die
  Selbstbedienung
sell verkaufen

sellotape (R) der Tesafilm (R)

send senden

sensible vernünftig

sensitive sensibel

separate(ly) getrennt

September der September

serious ernst

serve bedienen

service der Service

service charge die Bedienung

serviette die Serviette

several mehrere

sew nähen

sex der Sex; (gender) das Geschlecht

sexist sexistisch

sexy sexy

shade der Schatten

shampoo das Shampoo

share (verb) teilen·

shave sich rasieren

shaving brush der Rasierpinsel

shaving foam die Rasierseife

she sie

sheep das Schaf

sheet das Laken

shell die Muschel

shellfish die Schaltiere npl

ship das Schiff

shirt das Hemd

shock der Schock

shock-absorber der Stoßdämpfer

shocking skandalös

shoe laces die Schnürsenkel mpl

shoe polish die Schuhcreme

shoe repairer der Schuhmacher

shoes die Schuhe mpl

shop das Geschäft

shopping das Einkaufen; go

shopping einkaufen gehen

shopping bag die Einkaufstasche

shopping centre das Einkaufszentrum

shore das Ufer

short kurz

shortcut die Abkürzung

shorts die Shorts pl

shortsighted kurzsichtig

shoulder die Schulter

shout rufen

show (verb) zeigen

shower die Dusche; (rain) der Schauer

shutter (photo) der Verschluß

shutters (window) die Fensterläden mpl

shy scheu

sick: I feel sick mir ist schlecht; I'm going to be sick ich muß mich übergeben

side die Seite

sidelights das Standlicht

sign das Schild

sign (verb) unterschreiben

silence die Stille

silk die Seide

silver das Silber

silver foil die Alufolie

similar ähnlich

simple einfach

since (time) seit

sincere ehrlich

sing singen

single (unmarried) ledig

single room das Einzelzimmer

single ticket die einfache Fahrkarte

sink die Spüle

sink (go under) sinken

sister die Schwester
sister-in-law die Schwägerin
sit down sich setzen
size Größe
ski der Ski
ski (*verb*) skifahren
ski boots die Skistiefel *mpl*
skid schleudern
skiing das Skifahren
ski-lift der Skilift
skin die Haut
skin cleanser der
  Hautreiniger
skin-diving das
  Sporttauchen
skinny dünn
skirt der Rock
ski slope die Skipiste
skull der Schädel
sky der Himmel
sleep schlafen
sleeper der Schlafwagen
sleeping bag der Schlafsack
sleeping pill die
  Schlaftablette
sleepy müde
slice die Scheibe
slide (*photo*) das Dia
slim schlank
slippers die Hausschuhe *mpl*
slippery glatt
slow(ly) langsam
small klein
smell der Geruch
smell (*verb*) riechen
smile das Lächeln
smile (*verb*) lächeln
smoke der Rauch
smoke (*verb*) rauchen
smoking (*compartment*)
  Raucher
snack der Imbiß
snail die Schnecke

snake die Schlange
sneeze niesen
snore schnarchen
snow der Schnee
so so
soaking solution die
  Aufbewahrungslösung
soap die Seife
society die Gesellschaft
socket die Steckdose
socks die Socken *fpl*
soft weich
soft drink das alkoholfreie
  Getränk
soft lenses die weichen
  Kontaktlinsen *fpl*
sole (*of shoe*) die Sohle
some: some wine/flour etwas
  Wein/Mehl; **some biscuits**
  ein paar Plätzchen
somebody jemand
something etwas
sometimes manchmal
somewhere irgendwo
son der Sohn
song das Lied
son-in-law der
  Schwiegersohn
soon bald
sore: I've got a sore throat ich
  habe Halsschmerzen
sorry Entschuldigung!; **I'm
  sorry** tut mir leid
soup die Suppe
sour sauer
south der Süden; **south of**
  südlich von
souvenir das Souvenir
spade der Spaten
Spain Spanien
Spanish spanisch
spanner der
  Schraubenschlüssel

ENGLISH-GERMAN

spare parts die Ersatzteile *npl*
spare tyre der Ersatzreifen
spark plug die Zündkerze
speak sprechen; do you
  speak...? sprechen Sie...
speciality die Spezialität
speed die Geschwindigkeit
speed limit die Geschwin-
  digkeitsbeschränkung
speedometer der Tacho
spend ausgeben
spice das Gewürz
spider die Spinne
spinach der Spinat
spoke die Speiche
spoon der Löffel
sport der Sport
spot (*on skin*) der Pickel
sprain: I've sprained my
  ankle ich habe mir den Fuß
  verstaucht
spring (*season*) der Frühling;
  (*in seat etc*) die Feder
square (*in town*) der Platz
stain der Fleck
stairs die Treppe
stamp die Briefmarke
stand stehen; I can't stand
  cheese ich kann Käse nicht
  leiden
star der Stern
starter (*food*) die Vorspeise
state (*condition*) der Zustand
station der Bahnhof
stationer's der
  Schreibwarenladen
stay der Aufenthalt
stay (*remain*) bleiben; (*in hotel
  etc*) wohnen
steak das Steak
steal stehlen
steamer der Dampfer
steep steil

steering die Lenkung
steering wheel das Lenkrad
stepfather der Stiefvater
stepmother die Stiefmutter
steward der Steward
stewardess die Stewardeß
still (*adverb*) noch; (*not
  moving*) still
sting stechen
stockings die Strümpfe *mpl*
stomach der Magen
stomach ache die
  Magenschmerzen *mpl*
stone der Stein
stop (*bus-*) die Haltestelle
stop (*verb*) anhalten; stop!
  halt!
storm der Sturm
story die Geschichte
straight ahead geradeaus
strange (*odd*) seltsam
strawberry die Erdbeere
stream der Bach
street die Straße
string die Kordel
stroke (*attack*) der
  Schlaganfall
strong stark
stuck: it's stuck es klemmt
student der Student, die
  Studentin
stupid dumm
suburbs die Vorstadt
success der Erfolg
suddenly plötzlich
suede das Wildleder
sugar der Zucker
suit der Anzug
suit: blue suits you blau steht
  Ihnen
suitcase der Koffer
summer der Sommer
sun die Sonne

ENGLISH-GERMAN

sunbathe sonnenbaden
sunblock die Sun-Block-Creme
sunburn der Sonnenbrand
Sunday der Sonntag
sunglasses die Sonnenbrille
sunny sonnig
sunset der Sonnenuntergang
sunshine der Sonnenschein
sunstroke der Sonnenstich
suntan: you've got a good suntan du bist schön braun
suntan lotion das Sonnenöl
suntan oil das Sonnenöl
supermarket der Supermarkt
supplement der Zuschlag
sure sicher
surname der Nachname
surprise die Überraschung
surprising überraschend
swallow (*by accident*) verschlucken
sweat schwitzen
sweater der Pullover
sweet das Bonbon
sweet (*to taste*) süß
swim schwimmen
swimming das Schwimmen; **go swimming** schwimmen gehen
swimming costume der Badeanzug
swimming pool das Schwimmbad
swimming trunks die Badehose
Swiss Schweizer
switch der Schalter
switch off ausschalten
switch on anschalten
Switzerland die Schweiz
swollen geschwollen
synagogue die Synagoge

table der Tisch
tablecloth die Tischdecke
tablet die Tablette
table tennis das Tischtennis
tail der Schwanz
take nehmen; **take away** (*remove*) wegnehmen; **to take away** (*food*) zum Mitnehmen; **take off** (*plane*) abheben
talcum powder der Körperpuder
talk sprechen
tall groß
tampon das Tampon
tan (*colour*) die Bräune
tank der Tank
tap der Wasserhahn
tape (*cassette*) das Band
tart die Torte
taste der Geschmack
taste (*try*) probieren
taxi das Taxi
tea der Tee
teach: will you teach me some German können Sie mir etwas Deutsch beibringen?
teacher der Lehrer, die Lehrerin
team die Mannschaft
teapot die Teekanne
tea towel das Geschirrtuch
teenager der Teenager
telegram das Telegramm
telephone das Telefon
telephone directory das Telefonbuch
television das Fernsehen; **on**

television im Fernsehen;
watch television fernsehen
temperature die
Temperatur; (*medical*) das
Fieber
tennis das Tennis
tent das Zelt
tent peg der Hering
terrible furchtbar
terrific sagenhaft
than: uglier than häßlicher
als
thank danken
thank you danke
that (*adjective*) dieser, diese,
dieses; (*pronoun*) das; **I**
think that . . . ich glaube,
daß . . .; **that one** der/die/
das da
the der, die, das; *pl* die (*see*
grammar)
theatre das Theater
their ihr, ihre, ihr (*see*
grammar)
theirs: it's theirs es gehört
ihnen
them sie, ihnen
then dann
there da; **there is/are** es
gibt; **is/are there . . .?** gibt
es . . .?
thermometer das
Thermometer
thermos flask die
Thermosflasche
these diese
they sie
thick dick
thief der Dieb
thigh der Schenkel
thin dünn
thing das Ding
think denken

thirsty: I'm thirsty ich habe
Durst
this (*adjective*) dieser, diese,
dieses; (*pronoun*) dies,
das; **this one** dieser, diese,
dieses
those (*adjective*) die;
(*pronoun*) die
thread der Faden
throat die Kehle
throat pastilles die
Halstabletten *fpl*
through durch
throw werfen; **throw away**
wegwerfen
thunder der Donner
thunderstorm das Gewitter
Thursday der Donnerstag
ticket die Karte; (*for travel*)
die Fahrkarte
ticket office die Kasse;
(*trains etc*) der
Fahrkartenschalter
tide die Gezeiten *pl*
tie die Krawatte
tight eng
tights die Strumpfhose
time die Zeit; **two/three**
times zweimal/dreimal; **on**
time rechtzeitig; **what time**
is it? wie spät ist es?; **next**
time nächstes Mal
timetable der Fahrplan
tin opener der
Dosenöffner
tip das Trinkgeld
tired müde
tissues die Papiertücher *npl*
to: to Berlin/the bank nach
Berlin/zur Bank
toast der Toast
tobacco der Tabak
today heute

ENGLISH-GERMAN

toe die Zehe
together zusammen
toilet die Toilette
toilet paper das Toilettenpapier
tomato die Tomate
tomorrow morgen; **the day after tomorrow** übermorgen
tongue die Zunge
tonight heute abend
tonsillitis die Mandelentzündung
too (*also*) auch; **too big** zu groß; **not too much** nicht zu viel
tool das Werkzeug
tooth der Zahn
toothache die Zahnschmerzen *mpl*
toothbrush die Zahnbürste
toothpaste die Zahnpasta
top: at the top oben
torch die Taschenlampe
touch berühren
tourist der Tourist
towel das Handtuch
tower der Turm
town die Stadt
town hall das Rathaus
toy das Spielzeug
tracksuit der Trainingsanzug
tradition die Tradition
traditional traditionell
traffic der Verkehr
traffic jam der Stau
traffic lights die Ampel
traffic warden der Verkehrspolizist
trailer (*behind car*) der Anhänger
train der Zug
trainers die Turnschuhe *mpl*

tram die Straßenbahn
translate übersetzen
travel reisen
travel agent's das Reisebüro
traveller's cheque der Reisescheck
tray das Tablett
tree der Baum
tremendous fantastisch
trip der Ausflug
trolley der Kofferkuli
trousers die Hose
true wahr
try versuchen; **try on** anprobieren
T-shirt das T-Shirt
Tuesday der Dienstag
tuna fish der Thunfisch
tunnel der Tunnel
turkey der Truthahn
turn (*verb*) drehen; **turn off** abbiegen
tweezers die Pinzette
twins die Zwillinge
typewriter die Schreibmaschine
tyre der Reifen

ugly häßlich
umbrella der Schirm
uncle der Onkel
under unter
underdone nicht gar
underground die U-Bahn
underneath unten; **underneath ...** unter ...
underpants die Unterhose
understand verstehen

underwear die Unterwäsche
unemployed arbeitslos
unfortunately leider
United States die Vereinigten Staaten
university die Universität
unpack auspacken
unpleasant unangenehm
until bis
up: up there dort oben
upstairs oben
urgent dringend
us uns (*see grammar*)
use gebrauchen
useful nützlich
usual üblich
usually gewöhnlich

vaccination die Impfung
vacuum cleaner der Staubsauger
vagina die Vagina
valid gültig
valley das Tal
valve das Ventil
van der Kleinbus
vanilla die Vanille
vase die Vase
VD die Geschlechtskrankheit
veal das Kalbfleisch
vegetables das Gemüse
vegetarian vegetarisch
vehicle das Fahrzeug
very sehr
vet der Tierarzt
video das Video
video recorder der Videorecorder

view die Aussicht
viewfinder der Sucher
village das Dorf
vinegar der Essig
vineyard der Weinberg
visa das Visum
visit der Besuch
visit (*verb*) besuchen
vitamins die Vitamine *npl*
voice die Stimme

waist die Taille
wait warten; **wait for me!** warten Sie auf mich!
waiter der Kellner
waiting room der Wartesaal
waitress die Kellnerin
wake up (*someone*) wecken; (*oneself*) aufwachen
Wales Wales
walk der Spaziergang; **go for a walk** spazierengehen
walk (*verb*) gehen
walkman (*R*) der Walkman (*R*)
wall die Mauer; (*inside*) die Wand
wallet die Brieftasche
want wollen; **I want . . .** ich will . . .; **do you want . . .?** wollen Sie . . .?
war der Krieg
warm warm
wash waschen; (*oneself*) sich waschen
washbasin das Waschbecken
washing die Wäsche

washing machine die Waschmaschine
washing powder das Waschpulver
washing-up der Abwasch
washing-up liquid das Spülmittel
wasp die Wespe
watch (*for time*) die Armbanduhr
watch (*take care of*) aufpassen auf (*+acc*)
water das Wasser
waterfall der Wasserfall
waterskiing das Wasserski
wave (*in sea, hair*) die Welle
way: this way (*like this*) so; **can you tell me the way to the ...?** können Sie mir sagen, wie ich zum/zur ... komme?
we wir
weak schwach
weather das Wetter
weather forecast der Wetterbericht
wedding die Hochzeit
Wednesday der Mittwoch
week die Woche
weekend das Wochenende
weight das Gewicht
welcome! willkommen!
well: he's well/not well es geht ihm gut/schlecht
well (*adverb*) gut
well done durchgebraten
wellingtons die Gummistiefel *mpl*
Welsh walisisch
west der Westen; **west of** westlich von
wet naß
what? was?; **what ...?**

welcher/welche/welches ...?
wheel das Rad
wheelchair der Rollstuhl
when? wann?; **when I got here** als ich hier ankam
where? wo?
which? welcher?, welche?, welches?
while während
whipped cream die Schlagsahne
whisky der Whisky
white weiß
who? wer?; **the man who.../ woman who ...** der Mann, der .../die Frau, die ...
whole ganze
whooping cough der Keuchhusten
whose: whose is this? wem gehört das?
why? warum?
wide breit
widow die Witwe
widower der Witwer
wife die Frau
wild wild
win gewinnen
wind der Wind
window das Fenster
windscreen die Windschutzscheibe
windscreen wiper der Scheibenwischer
wine der Wein; **red/white/ rosé wine** der Rotwein/ Weißwein/Rosé
wine list die Weinkarte
wing der Flügel
winter der Winter
wire der Draht
wish: best wishes alles Gute

ENGLISH-GERMAN

with mit
without ohne
witness der Zeuge, die Zeugin
woman die Frau
wonderful wunderbar
wood das Holz
woods der Wald
wool die Wolle
word das Wort
work die Arbeit
work (*verb*) arbeiten; **it's not working** es funktioniert nicht
world die Welt
worry die Sorge
worry about sich Sorgen machen um
worse schlechter
worst: the worst der/die/das schlechteste
wound die Wunde
wrap einpacken
wrapping paper das Packpapier
wrench der Schraubenschlüssel
wrist das Handgelenk
write schreiben
writing paper das Schreibpapier
wrong falsch

yacht die Jacht
year das Jahr
yellow gelb
yes ja; **oh yes I do!** (*contradicting*) doch!
yesterday gestern; **the day before yesterday** vorgestern
yet: not yet noch nicht
yoghurt der Joghurt
you (*familiar*) du; (*plural*) ihr; (*polite, singular and plural*) Sie; **for you** für dich/euch/Sie; **with you** mit dir/euch/Ihnen (*see grammar*)
young jung; **young people** junge Leute
your (*familiar*) dein, deine, dein; (*plural*) euer, eure; (*polite, singular and plural*) Ihr, Ihre, Ihr (*see grammar*)
yours: it's yours (*familiar*) es gehört dir; (*plural*) es gehört euch; (*polite*) es gehört Ihnen (*see grammar*)
youth hostel die Jugendherberge

X-ray die Röntgenaufnahme

zero null
zip der Reißverschluß
zoo der Zoo

ab from; off; down
Abend *m* evening; **guten Abend** good evening; **zu Abend essen** have dinner
Abendessen *n* dinner
aber but
Abfahrt *f* departure
Abfall *m* litter; rubbish
Abfertigung *f* check-in
Abflug *m* departure
Abführmittel *n* laxative
abheben take off
Abkürzung *f* abbreviation; shortcut
abreisen leave
abschließen lock
absichtlich deliberately
Abstand *m* distance
Abteil *n* compartment
Abwasch *m* washing-up
Abzweigung *f* fork
Achse *f* axle
Achtung! look out!; attention
Adapter *m* adaptor
Adresse *f* address
Adreßbuch *n* address book
Agentur *f* agency
ähneln look like
ähnlich similar
Aktentasche *f* briefcase
Akzent *m* accent
akzeptieren accept
Algen *fpl* seaweed

alle: alle Milch/alles Bier all the milk/beer; **alle Männer/ Frauen** all men/women
allein alone
allergisch gegen allergic to
alles everything
Alptraum *m* nightmare
als when; than; as
alt old
Alter *n* age
Alufolie *f* silver foil
am at the, on (the)
Ameise *f* ant
Amerika *n* America
amerikanisch American
Ampel *f* traffic lights
amüsieren: sich amüsieren have fun
an on; **am Bahnhof** at the station
Ananas *f* pineapple
anbieten offer
andere another; **etwas anderes** something else
anderthalb one and a half
Anfang *m* beginning
anfangen begin
Anfänger *m* beginner
Angeln *n* fishing
angenehm pleasant
Angst *f* fear; **ich habe Angst (vor)** I'm afraid (of)
anhalten stop
Anhänger *m* trailer
Anker *m* anchor
ankommen arrive; **das kommt darauf an** it depends

Ankunft f arrival
anprobieren try on
anrufen phone; ring
ans to the
anschalten switch on
Anschluß m connection
Anschrift f address
ansehen look (at)
Antiquitätenladen m antique shop
Antwort f answer
antworten answer
anziehen dress; **sich anziehen** dress
Anzug m suit
anzünden light
Apfel m apple
Apfelkuchen m apple pie
Apfelwein m cider
Apotheke f chemist's
Appetit m appetite; **guten Appetit** enjoy your meal!
Aprikose f apricot
Arbeit f work; job
arbeiten work
arbeitslos unemployed
ärgerlich annoying
Arm m arm
arm poor
Armaturenbrett n dashboard
Armband n bracelet
Armbanduhr f watch
Arzt m doctor
Aschenbecher m ashtray
atmen breathe
auch too, also; **ich auch** me too
auf on; open; **auf englisch** in English
Aufbewahrungslösung f soaking solution
Aufenthalt m stay
aufgeben give up; post

aufpassen auf take care of; watch out for
aufregend exciting
aufstehen get up
aufwachen wake up
auf Wiedersehen goodbye
Aufzug m lift
Auge n eye
Augenarzt m optician
Augenblick m moment
Augenbraue f eyebrow
aus from; off; out; out of; finished
Ausflug m trip
Ausgang m exit
ausgeben spend
ausgezeichnet excellent
Auskunft f information; information desk; directory enquiries
Ausland n: **im/ins Ausland** abroad
Ausländer m foreigner
ausländisch foreign
auspacken unpack
Auspuff m exhaust
ausruhen: sich ausruhen relax; take a rest
ausschalten switch off
außen outside
außer except
außerdem besides
Aussicht f view
aussprechen pronounce
aussteigen get off
Ausstellung f exhibition
Auster f oyster
Australien n Australia
australisch Australian
Ausverkauf m sale
Auto n car
Autobahn f motorway
Autofahrer m car driver

GERMAN-ENGLISH

automatisch automatic
Autovermietung *f* car rental

B

Bach *m* stream
backen bake
Bäckerei *f* baker's
Backofen *m* oven
Backstein *m* brick
Bad *n* bath
Badeanzug *m* swimming
costume
Badehose *f* swimming trunks
Badekappe *f* bathing cap
Bademantel *m* dressing
gown
Badesalz *n* bath salts
Badewanne *f* bathtub
Badezimmer *n* bathroom
Bahnhof *m* station
Bahnsteig *m* platform
Bahnübergang *m* level
crossing
bald soon
Balkon *m* balcony
Ball *m* ball
Banane *f* banana
Band *n* tape
Bank *f* bank; bench
bar: bar zahlen pay cash
Bardame *f* barmaid
Bart *m* beard
Batterie *f* battery
Bauer *m* farmer
Bauernhof *m* farm
Baum *m* tree
Baumwolle *f* cotton
Beamter *m* civil servant;
official

bedeuten mean
bedienen serve
Bedienung *f* service (charge)
beeilen: sich beeilen hurry;
beeilen Sie sich! hurry up!
beenden finish
Beerdigung *f* funeral
befehlen order
begleiten accompany
behalten keep
behindert disabled
bei: bei Wolfgang at
Wolfgang's
beide both (of them)
Beil *n* axe
Bein *n* leg
beinahe almost
Beispiel *n* example; **zum
Beispiel** for example
bekommen get
beleidigen offend
Belgien *n* Belgium
belgisch Belgian
Belichtungsmesser *m* light
meter
Benzin *n* petrol
Benzinuhr *f* fuel gauge
beobachten watch
bequem comfortable
bereit ready
Berg *m* mountain
Bergsteigen *n*
mountaineering
beruhigen: sich beruhigen
calm down
berühmt famous
berühren touch
beschädigen damage
Bescheid *m* information; **er
weiß Bescheid** he knows
(about it)
Bescheinigung *f* certificate
beschweren: sich

beschweren complain
Besen *m* broom
besetzt busy; engaged
Besichtigung *f* tour
Besitzer *m* owner
besonders especially
besser better
Besserung *f*: **gute Besserung** get well soon
bestätigen confirm
beste best
Besteck *n* cutlery
Bestellung *f* order
Besuch *m* visit
besuchen visit
Besuchszeit *f* visiting time
Betrieb *m*: **außer Betrieb** out of order
betrunken drunk
Bett *n* bed
Bettwäsche *f* bed linen
bewegen: sich bewegen move
bewölkt cloudy
BH *m* bra
Biene *f* bee
Bier *n* beer
Bild *n* picture
billig cheap
Birne *f* pear; light bulb
bis until; **bis morgen** see you tomorrow
bißchen: ein bißchen a little bit (of)
Bissen *m* bite
bitte please; **bitte?** pardon?
bitter bitter
Bitterschokolade *f* plain chocolate
Blase *f* bladder; blister
Blatt *n* leaf
blau blue; **blauer Fleck** bruise

bleiben stay, remain
Bleichmittel *n* bleach
Bleistift *m* pencil
Blinddarmentzündung *f* appendicitis
Blinker *m* indicator
Blitz *m* flash
blockiert blocked
bloß bare; only
Blume *f* flower
Blumenhandlung *f* florist
Blumenkohl *m* cauliflower
Bluse *f* blouse
Blut *n* blood
bluten bleed
Blutgruppe *f* blood group
Boden *m* bottom; floor
Bohnen *fpl* beans
Boje *f* buoy
Bombe *f* bomb
Bonbon *n* sweet
Bordkarte *f* boarding pass
böse angry
Botschaft *f* embassy
braten fry
Bratpfanne *f* frying pan
Brauch *m* custom
brauchen need
braun brown
breit wide
Bremse *f* brake
bremsen brake
brennen burn
Brief *m* letter
Briefkasten *m* letterbox
Briefmarke *f* stamp
Brieftasche *f* wallet
Briefträger *m* postman
Brille *f* glasses
bringen bring
britisch British
Brombeere *f* blackberry
Brosche *f* brooch

GERMAN-ENGLISH

Broschüre f brochure
Brot n bread; **belegtes Brot** sandwich
Brötchen n roll
Bruch m fracture
Brücke f bridge
Bruder m brother
Brunnen m fountain
Brust f breast; chest
Buch n book
buchen book
Bücherei f library
Buchhandlung f bookshop
Bügeleisen n iron
bügeln iron
bunt coloured; colourful
Burg f castle
Bürgersteig m pavement
Büro n office
Bürste f brush
Busbahnhof m bus station
Bushaltestelle f bus stop
bzw. or

Campingliege f campbed
Campingplatz m campsite; caravan site
Charterflug m charter flight
Chauvi m male chauvinist pig
Chef m boss
chemische Reinigung f dry-cleaner
Chips pl crisps

da there; as; since
Dach n roof
Dachgepäckträger m roof rack
Dame f lady
Damenbinde f sanitary towel
Dampfer m steamer
dankbar grateful
danke thank you
danken thank
dann then
das the; which; that
daß that
Datum n date
Dauerwelle f perm
Decke f blanket; ceiling
Deckel m lid
dein, deine your
denken think
Denkmal n monument
deprimiert depressed
der, die, das; pl **die** the; who; that; **der/die/das da** that one
Desinfektionsmittel n disinfectant
deutsch German
Deutsche m/f German
Deutschland Germany
Dezember m December
d.h. i.e.
Dia n slide
Diamant m diamond
Diät f diet
dich you
dick fat; thick
die the; which; that
Dieb m thief

Dienstag *m* Tuesday
dies, diese that/this (one), these (ones)
dieser, dieses that/this (one)
Ding *n* thing
dir (to) you
doch! oh yes it is/I am *etc*
Dom *m* cathedral
Donner *m* thunder
Donnerstag *m* Thursday
doof stupid
Doppelbett *n* double bed
doppelt double
Doppelzimmer *n* double room
Dorf *n* village
dort there; **dort drüben/oben** over/up there
Dose *f* can
Dosenöffner *m* tin opener
Draht *m* wire
Drahtseilbahn *f* cable car
drehen turn
dringend urgent
Drittel *n* third
Droge *f* drug
Drogerie *f* chemist's
drücken push
Drucksache *f* printed matter
du you
dumm stupid
Dünen *fpl* sand dunes
dunkel dark
dünn thin; skinny
durch through; by; well-done
Durcheinander *n* mess
Durchfall *m* diarrhoea
durchgebraten well done
dürfen be allowed to
Durst *m*: **ich habe Durst** I'm thirsty
Dusche *f* shower

Duty-free-Laden *m* duty-free shop

echt genuine
Ecke *f* corner
EG *f* EEC
ehe before
Ehefrau *f* wife
Ehemann *m* husband
ehrlich honest; sincere
Ei *n* egg; **gekochtes Ei** boiled egg; **hartgekochtes Ei** hard-boiled egg
Eierbecher *m* egg cup
eifersüchtig jealous
eigentlich actual(ly)
Eimer *m* bucket
ein, eine a; one
einfach simple; single
Eingang *m* entrance
einige a few
Einkauf *m* shopping
einkaufen: einkaufen gehen go shopping
Einkaufstasche *f* shopping bag
Einkaufszentrum *n* shopping centre
einladen invite
Einladung *f* invitation
einmal once
einpacken wrap
eins one
einsteigen get in
eintreten in enter
Eintrittskarte *f* ticket
einverstanden! OK
Einzelbett *n* single bed

Einzelfahrkarte f single ticket

Einzelzimmer n single room

Eis n ice; ice cream; **Eis am Stiel** ice lolly

Eisen n iron

Eisenbahn f railway

Eisenwarenhandlung f ironmonger's

elastisch elastic

elektrisch electric

Elektrizität f electricity

Ellbogen m elbow

Eltern pl parents

empfehlen recommend

Ende n end

endlich at last

eng narrow; tight

Engländer m, **Engländerin** f Englishman; English girl/woman

englisch English; rare

Ente f duck

entscheiden decide

entschuldigen: sich entschuldigen apologize

Entschuldigung! excuse me; sorry

entsetzlich appalling

enttäuscht disappointed

entweder ... oder ... either ... or ...

entwickeln develop

Entzündung f infection

er he

Erbsen fpl peas

Erdbeere f strawberry

Erde f earth

Erdgeschoß n ground floor

Erdnüsse fpl peanuts

Erfolg m success

erhalten receive

erinnern: sich erinnern an remember

erkältet: ich bin erkältet I've got a cold

Erkältung f cold

erkennen recognize

erklären explain

erlauben allow

ernst serious

Ersatzreifen m spare tyre

Ersatzteile npl spare parts

erstatten refund

erstaunlich astonishing

erste first; **Erste Hilfe** first aid

Erwachsene m/f adult

es it

Esel m donkey

essen eat

Essen n food

Essig m vinegar

Etage f floor, storey

Etagenbett n bunk beds

Etikett n label

etwa about

etwas something; **etwas Wein/Mehl** some wine/flour

euch you

euer, eure your

Europa n Europe

europäisch European

Euroscheck m Eurocheque

evangelisch Protestant

Fabrik f factory

Faden m string; thread

Fahne f flag

Fähre f ferry

fahren drive
Fahrer m driver
Fahrkarte f ticket
Fahrkartenschalter m ticket office
Fahrplan m timetable
Fahrrad n bicycle
Fahrstuhl m lift
Fahrt f journey
Fahrzeug n vehicle
fallen fall
fallenlassen drop
falls if
falsch wrong; false
Familie f family
fangen catch
fantastisch tremendous
Farbe f colour
Farbfilm m colour film
fast almost, nearly
faul lazy; rotten
Februar m February
Feder f feather; spring
Federbett n quilt
Fehler m mistake
fehlerhaft faulty
Feiertag m holiday
Feld n field
Felsen m rock
feministisch feminist
Fenster n window
Fensterläden mpl shutters
Ferien pl holidays
Fernsehen n television
Ferse f heel
fertig ready
festnehmen arrest
Fete f party
Fett n fat
fett greasy
feucht damp
Feuchtigkeitscreme f moisturizer; cold cream

Feuer n fire; **haben Sie Feuer?** have you got a light?
Feuerlöscher m fire extinguisher
Feuerwehr f fire brigade
Feuerwerk n fireworks
Feuerzeug n lighter
Fieber n fever
Filet n fillet
Filzstift m felt-tip pen
finden find
Fingernagel m fingernail
Firma f company
Fisch n fish
Fischgeschäft n fishmonger's
flach flat
Flasche f bottle
Flaschenöffner m bottle-opener
Fleck m stain
Fleisch n meat
Fliege f fly
fliegen fly
flirten flirt
Flitterwochen fpl honeymoon
Floh m flea
Flug m flight
Flügel m wing
Flughafen m airport
Fluglinie f airline
Flugzeug n (aero)plane
Flur m corridor
Fluß m river
folgen follow
folgende next
Folk m folk music
Fön (R) m hair dryer
fönen: sich fönen lassen to have a blow-dry
fordern demand
Formular n form
Foto n photograph

Fotograf *m* photographer
fotografieren photograph
Frage *f* question
fragen ask
Frankreich *n* France
Franzose *m*, **Französin** *f*
Frenchman, French girl/
woman
französisch French
Frau *f* woman; wife; Mrs; Ms
Fräulein *n* Miss
frei free
Freitag *m* Friday
freuen: sich freuen be
happy; **freut mich!** pleased
to meet you!
Freund *m* friend; boyfriend
Freundin *f* friend; girlfriend
freundlich kind
Friedhof *m* cemetery
frisch fresh
Friseur *m* barber;
hairdresser
Frl. Miss
froh glad; **frohe**
Weihnachten! happy
Christmas!; **frohes neues**
Jahr happy New Year!
Frostschutzmittel *n*
antifreeze
früh early
Frühling *m* spring
Frühstück *n* breakfast
fühlen feel; **ich fühle mich**
gut/schlecht I feel well/
unwell
Führerschein *m* driving
licence
füllen fill
Fundbüro *n* lost property
office
funktionieren work
für for

furchtbar terrible
Fuß *m* foot; **zu Fuß** on foot
Fußball *m* football
Fußgänger *m* pedestrian
Fußgängerüberweg *m*
pedestrian crossing
Fußgängerzone *f* pedestrian
precinct

Gabel *f* fork
Gang *m* gear
Gans *f* goose
ganz whole; quite; **den**
ganzen Tag all day; **ganz**
gut pretty good; **ganz naß**
all wet
gar cooked; **nicht gar**
underdone
Garantie *f* guarantee
Garderobe *f* cloakroom
Garten *m* garden
Gaspedal *n* accelerator
Gast *m* guest
Gastfreundschaft *f*
hospitality
Gaststätte *f* inn, pub
Gebäude *n* building
geben give; **es gibt . . .** there
is/are . . .; **gibt es . . .?** is/are
there . . .?
Gebiß *n* dentures
geboren: ich bin 1963
geboren I was born in 1963
gebrauchen use
gebraucht second-hand
Gebühr *f* fee, charge
Geburtstag *m* birthday; **viel**
Glück zum Geburtstag

happy birthday
Gefahr f danger
gefährlich dangerous
Gefängnis n prison
Geflügel n poultry
Gefriertruhe f freezer
gefroren frozen
Gefühl n feeling
gegen against
Gegend f area
Gegenteil n opposite
gegenüber: gegenüber der Kirche opposite the church
gegrillt grilled
geheim secret
gehen go; walk; **es geht ihm gut/schlecht** he's well/not well; **mir geht's gut** I'm OK; **wie geht es Ihnen?** how are you?; **wie geht's?** how are things?
gehören belong (to)
Geistliche m priest
gelb yellow
Geld n money
Geldautomat m cash dispenser
Geldschein m banknote
Geldstrafe f fine
Gemälde n painting
Gemüse n vegetable(s)
Gemüsehändler m greengrocer
Genehmigung f licence
genug enough; **ich habe genug (von)** I'm fed up (with)
geöffnet open
Gepäck n luggage
Gepäckaufbewahrung f left luggage
geradeaus straight ahead
Gerät n device

gerecht fair
Geruch m smell
Geschäft n shop; business
Geschäftsführer m manager
Geschäftsreise f business trip
geschehen happen
Geschenk n present
Geschichte f story; history
geschieden divorced
Geschirr n crockery
Geschirrtuch n tea towel
Geschlecht n sex
Geschlechtskrankheit f VD
geschlossen closed
Geschmack m taste; flavour
Geschwindigkeit f speed
Geschwindigkeitsbeschränkung f speed limit
geschwollen swollen
Gesellschaft f society
Gesetz n law
Gesicht n face
gesperrt closed
gestattet allowed
gestern yesterday
gesund healthy
Gesundheit f health; **Gesundheit!** bless you!
getrennt separate(ly)
Getriebe n gearbox
Gewehr n gun
Gewicht n weight
gewinnen win
Gewitter n thunderstorm
Gewohnheit f habit
gewöhnlich usually
Gewürz n spice
Gezeiten pl tide
Gift n poison
Gitarre f guitar
Glas n glass
glatt slippery
glauben believe

Gleis n platform
Glocke f bell
Glück n luck; **viel Glück!** good luck!; **zum Glück** fortunately
glücklich happy
Glühbirne f light bulb
Gott m God
Gottesdienst m mass
Grammatik f grammar
Gras n grass
Gräte f fishbone
gratis free
grau grey
Grenze f border
Griechenland n Greece
griechisch Greek
Griff m handle
Grippe f flu
groß big, large; tall
Großbritannien n Great Britain
Größe f size
Großmutter f grandmother
Großvater m grandfather
grün green; **grüne Bohnen** green beans
Grund m cause
Grundierungscreme f foundation cream
Gruppe f group; party
Gruß m greeting
grüßen greet; say hello to; **grüß Gott** hello
gültig valid
Gummi n rubber
Gummiband n rubber band
Gummistiefel mpl wellingtons
günstig favourable; convenient; inexpensive
Gurke f cucumber
Gürtel m belt

gut good; well; **alles Gute** best wishes
gutaussehend handsome

Haar n hair
Haarfestiger m conditioner
Haarschnitt m haircut
Haarspray n hair spray
haben have
Hackfleisch n minced meat
Hafen m harbour
Hagel m hail
Hähnchen n chicken
halb half
Halbpension f half board
Hälfte f half
Hals n neck
Halskette f necklace
Halsschmerzen mpl sore throat
Halstabletten fpl throat pastilles
halt! stop!
halten hold; stop
Haltestelle f stop
Hämorrhoiden pl piles
Hand f hand
Handbremse f handbrake
Handgelenk n wrist
Handgepäck n hand luggage
Handschuhe mpl gloves
Handtasche f handbag
Handtuch n towel
Handwerk n crafts
Handzettel m leaflet
Hansaplast (R) n Elastoplast (R)
hart hard

Haselnuß *f* hazelnut
hassen hate
häßlich ugly
Haupt- main
Hauptsaison *f* high season
Haus *n* house; **nach Hause gehen** go home; **zu Hause** at home
hausgemacht homemade
Hausschuhe *mpl* slippers
Haut *f* skin
Hautreiniger *m* skin cleanser
Heimweh *n*: **ich habe Heimweh** I'm homesick
heiß hot
heißen: ich heiße Jim my name is Jim; **wie heißen Sie?** what's your name?
Heizgerät *n* heater
Heizung *f* heating
helfen help
hell light; bright
Hemd *n* shirt
Herbst *m* autumn
Herd *m* cooker
herein! come in!
Herr *m* gentleman; **Herr Jones** Mr Jones
herrlich lovely
Herz *n* heart
Herzinfarkt *m* heart attack
herzlich: herzlichen Glückwunsch! congratulations!
Heufieber *n* hay fever
heute today; **heute abend** tonight
hier here
Hilfe *f* help
Himbeere *f* raspberry
Himmel *m* sky
hinlegen: sich hinlegen lie down

hinten at the back
hinter behind
Hintern *n* bottom
Hinterrad *n* back wheel
hoch high
Hochzeit *f* wedding
Hochzeitstag *m* wedding anniversary
hoffen hope
höflich polite
Höhle *f* cave
holländisch Dutch
Holz *n* wood
Honig *m* honey
hören hear
Hörgerät *n* hearing aid
Höschen *n* panties
Hose *f* trousers
hübsch pretty
Hubschrauber *m* helicopter
Hüfte *f* hip
Hügel *m* hill
Huhn *n* chicken
Hummer *m* lobster
Humor *m* humour
Hund *m* dog
Hunger *m*: **ich habe Hunger** I'm hungry
Hupe *f* horn
Husten *f* cough
husten cough
Hut *f* hat

ich I
Idee *f* idea
ihm him
ihn him
ihnen them

GERMAN-ENGLISH

ihr you; her
ihr, ihre her; their
Ihr, Ihre your
im in (the)
Imbiß *m* snack
immer always
Impfung *f* vaccination
in in
inbegriffen included
Industrie *f* industry
innen (im/in) inside
ins in(to) the
Insektenschutzmittel *n*
  insect repellent
Insel *f* island
insgesamt altogether
interessant interesting
irgendwo somewhere
irisch Irish
Irland *n* Ireland
Italien *n* Italy
italienisch Italian

ja yes
Jacht *f* yacht
Jacke *f* jacket; cardigan
Jahr *n* year
Jahreszeit *f* season
Jahrhundert *n* century
Jahrmarkt *m* fair
Januar *m* January
jede each; every; **jeden Tag**
  every day
jeder everyone
jedesmal every time
jemand somebody
jetzt now
joggen: joggen gehen go

  jogging
Jucken *n* itch
jüdisch Jewish
Jugendherberge *f* youth
  hostel
Juli *m* July
jung young; **junge Leute**
  young people
Junge *m* boy
Junggeselle *m* bachelor
Juni *m* June
Juwelier *m* jeweller's

Kabine *f* cabin
Kaffee *m* coffee; **Kaffee mit
  Milch** white coffee
kahl bald
Kai *m* quay
Kakao *m* cocoa; hot
  chocolate
Kalbfleisch *n* veal
Kalender *m* calendar
kalt cold
Kamera *f* camera
Kamm *m* comb
Kampf *m* fight
kämpfen fight
Kanada *n* Canada
kanadisch Canadian
Kanal *m* canal; Channel
Kaninchen *n* rabbit
Kanu *n* canoe
Kapitän *m* captain
kaputt broken
Karte *f* card
Kartoffel *f* potato
Käse *m* cheese
Kasse *f* cash desk; box office
Kassette *f* cassette

Kastanie *f* chestnut
Kater *m* tomcat; hangover
katholisch Catholic
Katze *f* cat
kaufen buy
Kaufhaus *n* department store
Kaugummi *m* chewing gum
Kehle *f* throat
Keilriemen *m* fan belt
kein, keine no; kein(e) ... mehr no more ...; ich habe keine I don't have any
Kellner *m* waiter
Kellnerin *f* waitress
kennen know
Kerze *f* candle
Kette *f* chain
Keuchhusten *m* whooping cough
Kiefer *m* jaw
Kind *n* child
Kinderbett *n* cot
Kinderteller *m* children's portion
Kinderwagen *m* pram
Kinn *n* chin
Kino *n* cinema
Kirche *f* church
Kirsche *f* cherry
klar clear
Klasse *f* class; erste/zweite Klasse first/second class
Kleid *n* dress
Kleider *pl* clothes
Kleiderbügel *m* (coat)hanger
klein small
Kleinbus *m* van
Kleingeld *n* change
Klempner *m* plumber
Klima *n* climate
Klimaanlage *f* air-conditioning

Klingel *f* bell
Klippe *f* cliff
klug clever
Kneipe *f* pub
Knie *n* knee
Knoblauch *m* garlic
Knöchel *m* ankle
Knochen *m* bone
Knopf *m* button
Koch *m* cook
kochen cook; boil
Kochgeschirr *n* cooking utensils
Kochtopf *m* saucepan
koffeinfrei decaffeinated
Koffer *m* bag; suitcase
Kofferkuli *m* luggage trolley
Kofferraum *m* boot
Kohl *m* cabbage
komisch funny
kommen come
Kompaß *m* compass
Kompliment *n* compliment
kompliziert complicated
Konditorei *f* cake shop
König *m* king
Königin *f* queen
können: ich/sie kann I/she can; können Sie ... can you ...?
Konsulat *n* consulate
Kontaktlinsen *fpl* contact lenses
Konzert *n* concert
Kopf *m* head
Kopfkissen *n* pillow
Kopfschmerzmittel *n* aspirin
Kopftuch *n* scarf
Kopfweh *n* basket
Korkenzieher *m* corkscrew
Körper *m* body
Körperpuder *m* talcum powder

kosten cost
köstlich delicious
Kotelett n chop
Krabbe f crab; prawn
Kragen m collar
Krampf m cramp
krank ill
Krankenhaus n hospital
Krankenschwester f nurse
Krankenwagen m ambulance
Krankheit f disease
Kräuter npl herbs
Krawatte f tie
Kreditkarte f credit card
Kreisverkehr m roundabout
Kreuzfahrt f cruise
Kreuzung f junction
Krieg m war
kriegen get
Krücken fpl crutches
Krug m jug
Küche f kitchen; cuisine
Kuchen m cake; pie
Küchenschabe f cockroach
Kugel f ball
Kugelschreiber m biro (R)
Kuh f cow
kühl cool
Kühler m radiator
Kühlschrank m fridge
Kunst f art
Kunstgalerie f art gallery
Künstler m artist
künstlich artificial
Kupplung f clutch
Kurbelwelle f crankshaft
Kurve f bend
kurz short
kurzsichtig shortsighted
Kusine f cousin
Kuß m kiss
küssen kiss
Küste f coast

Lächeln n smile
lächeln smile
lachen laugh
lächerlich ridiculous
Lachs m salmon
Laden m shop
Laken n sheet
Lamm n Lamb
Lampe f lamp
Land n country
landen land
Landkarte f map
Landschaft f countryside; landscape; scenery
lang long
Länge f length
langsam slow(ly)
Languste f crayfish
langweilig boring
Lärm m noise
lassen let; leave
Lastwagen m lorry
laufen run
Läufer m runner; rug
laut loud; noisy
lauwarm lukewarm
Leben n life
leben live
lebendig alive
Lebensgefahr f danger
Lebensmittelhandlung f grocer's
Lebensmittelvergiftung f food poisoning
Leber f liver
Leck n leak
Leder n leather
ledig single

GERMAN-ENGLISH

leer empty
Lehrer *m* teacher; instructor
leicht easy; light
leid: tut mir leid I'm sorry
leiden suffer; **ich kann Käse
nicht leiden** I can't stand
cheese
leider unfortunately
leihen borrow; lend
Leim *m* glue
Leiter *f* ladder
Lenkrad *n* steering wheel
Lenkung *f* steering
lernen learn
lesen read
letzte last
Leuchtturm *m* lighthouse
Leute *pl* people
Licht *n* light
Lichtmaschine *f* alternator
Lidschatten *m* eye shadow
Liebe *f* love
lieben love
Lieblings- favourite
Lied *n* song
Liegestuhl *m* deck chair
Liegewagen *f* couchette
Likör *m* liqueur
Limonade *f* lemonade
links left; **links (von)** on the
left (of)
linkshändig left-handed
Linse *f* lens; lentil
Lippe *f* lip
Lippenstift *m* lipstick
Liste *f* list
Loch *n* hole
Löffel *m* spoon
Lokomotive *f* engine
Luft *f* air
Luftpost *f*: **per Luftpost** by
airmail
lügen lie

Lunge *f* lungs
Lungenentzündung *f*
pneumonia
Lust *f*: **ich habe Lust auf** I
feel like
Lutscher *m* lollipop

machen make; **das macht
nichts** it doesn't matter
Mädchen *n* girl
Mädchenname *m* maiden
name
Magazin *n* magazine
Magen *m* stomach
Magenschmerzen *mpl*
stomach ache
Magenverstimmung *f*
indigestion
Mahlzeit *f* meal
Mai *m* May
Mal *n* time; **zum ersten Mal**
for the first time
man one; you; **man sagt,
daß ...** they say that ...
manchmal sometimes
Mandelentzündung *f*
tonsillitis
Mann *m* man; husband
Mannschaft *f* team; crew
Mantel *m* coat
Markt *m* market
Marmelade *f* jam
März *m* March
Masern *pl* measles
Matratze *f* mattress
Mauer *f* wall
Maus *f* mouse
Mechaniker *m* mechanic

105

Medizin f medicine
Meer n sea; **am Meer** at the seaside
Meeresfrüchte fpl seafood
Mehl n flour
mehr more
mehrere several
Mehrfachstecker m adaptor
mein, meine my
meiste: das meiste (von) most (of)
Melone f melon
Menge f crowd
Mensch m person
Menü n set menu
Messe f (trade) fair
Messer n knife
Metall n metal
Meter m metre
Metzger m butcher's
mich me
Miete f rent
mieten rent
Milch f milk
mindestens at least
Mineralwasser n mineral water
mischen mix
Mißverständnis n misunderstanding
mit with; **mit dem Auto** by car
mitnehmen take; give a lift to; **zum Mitnehmen** to take away
Mittag m midday
Mittagessen n lunch
Mitte f middle
Mittelalter n Middle Ages
mittelgroß medium-sized
Mittelmeer n Mediterranean
Mitternacht f midnight
Mittwoch m Wednesday

Möbel pl furniture
Mode f fashion
modisch fashionable
mögen like; **ich möchte gern** I would like
möglich possible
Mohrrübe f carrot
Monat m month
Mond m moon
Montag m Monday
Morgen m morning; **guten Morgen** good morning
morgen tomorrow
Motor m engine
Motorboot n motorboat
Motorhaube f bonnet
Motorrad n motorbike
Möwe f seagull
müde tired
Mülltonne f dustbin
Mund m mouth
Muschel f shell
Muscheln fpl mussels
Musik f music
Musikinstrument n musical instrument
Muskel m muscle
müssen have to; **ich muß/sie muß** I/she must
mutig brave
Mutter f mother; nut
Mutti f mum
Mütze f cap

nach after; **ich fahre nach Berlin/Schottland** I'm going to Berlin/Scotland
Nachbar m neighbour

nachher afterwards
Nachmittag *m* afternoon
Nachname *m* surname
Nachricht *f* message
Nachrichten *fpl* news
nachsenden forward
nächste next; **der/die/das nächste ...** the nearest ...; **nächstes Jahr** next year
Nacht *f* night; **gute Nacht** good night
Nachthemd *n* nightdress
Nachtisch *m* dessert
Nachtklub *m* nightclub
nackt naked
Nadel *f* needle; pin
Nagel *m* nail
Nagelfeile *f* nailfile
Nagellack *m* nail polish
Nagellackentferner *m* nail polish remover
Nagelschere *f* nail clippers
nah(e) near
Nähe *f*: **in der Nähe** near here
nähen sew
Name *m* name
Nase *f* nose
naß wet
Natur *f* nature
natürlich natural; of course
Nebel *m* fog
neben next to
Neffe *m* nephew
nehmen take
nein no
Nervenzusammenbruch *m* nervous breakdown
nervös nervous
nett nice
neu new
Neujahr *n* New Year
neurotisch neurotic

nicht not; do not
Nichte *f* niece
Nichtraucher non-smoking
nichts nothing
nie never
niemand nobody
Niere *f* kidney
niesen sneeze
nirgends nowhere
noch still; **noch ein Bier** another beer; **noch nicht** not yet; **noch schöner** even more beautiful
nochmal again
Norden *m* north
Nordirland *n* Northern Ireland
nördlich von north of
Notausgang *m* emergency exit
Notfall *m* emergency
nötig necessary
Notizbuch *n* notebook
notwendig necessary
Nudeln *fpl* pasta
null zero
Nummer *f* number
Nummernschild *n* number plate
nun now
nur only; just
Nuß *f* nut
nützlich useful

ob whether
oben at the top; upstairs
Obst *n* fruit
obwohl although
oder or

offen open
offensichtlich obvious
öffentlich public
öffnen open
oft often
ohne without
Ohnmacht f: in Ohnmacht fallen faint
Ohr n ear
Ohrringe mpl earrings
Öl n oil
Olivenöl n olive oil
Onkel m uncle
Oper f opera
optimistisch optimistic
Ordnung f order; in Ordnung all right
organisieren organize
Ort m place
Osten m east
Ostern Easter
Österreich n Austria
östlich von east of
Ostsee f Baltic

Paar n pair
paar: ein paar ... a few ...
packen pack
Packpapier n wrapping paper
Paket n parcel; package
Palast m palace
Pampelmuse f grapefruit
Panik f panic
Panne f breakdown; eine Panne haben break down
Papier n paper
Papiertücher npl tissues

Pappe f cardboard
Paprikaschote f pepper
Parfüm n perfume
parken park
Parkhaus n multi-storey carpark
Parkplatz m car park
Paß m passport; pass
Passagier m passenger
Pastete f pâté
Pauschalreise f package tour
peinlich embarrassing
Pension f guesthouse
Pfannkuchen m pancake
Pfeffer m pepper
Pfeife f pipe
Pferd n horse
Pfirsich m peach
Pflanze f plant
Pflaume f plum
Pfund n pound
Pickel m spot
pikant savoury
Pille f pill
Pilze mpl mushrooms
Pinsel m paint brush
Pinzette f tweezers
Pistole f gun
Pkw m car
Plakat n poster
Plastik n plastic
Plastiktüte f plastic bag
platt flat
Plattenspieler m record player
Platz m seat; square
Plätzchen n biscuit
pleite broke
Plombe f filling
plötzlich suddenly
politisch political
Polizei f police
Polizeiwache f police station

GERMAN-ENGLISH

Polizist *m* policeman
Pommes frites *pl* chips
Portemonnaie *n* purse
Portier *m* porter
Portwein *m* port
Post *f* mail; post office
Postkarte *f* postcard
postlagernd poste restante
Postleitzahl *f* postcode
praktisch practical
Präservativ *n* durex (R)
Preis *m* price
preiswert inexpensive
prima! good!
Prinz *m* prince
Prinzessin *f* princess
pro: pro Woche per week
probieren try
prost! cheers!
Prozent *n* per cent
prüfen check
Publikum *n* audience
Pulverkaffee *m* instant coffee
Pumpe *f* pump
Puppe *f* doll

Qualität *f* quality
Qualle *f* jellyfish
Quatsch *m* nonsense
Quittung *f* receipt

Rabatt *m* reduction, discount
Rad *n* wheel
Radfahren *n* cycling
Radfahrer *m* cyclist
Radiergummi *m* rubber
Rasen *m* lawn
Raslerapparat *m* razor
rasieren: sich rasieren shave
Rasierklinge *f* razor blade
Rasierpinsel *m* shaving
  brush
Rasierseife *f* shaving foam
Rasierwasser *n* aftershave
Raststätte *f* services area
raten guess; advise
Rathaus *n* town hall
Ratte *f* rat
Rauch *m* smoke
rauchen smoke
Raucher smoking
raus! get out!
Rechnung *f* bill
rechts right; **rechts (von)** on
  the right (of)
Rechtsanwalt *m* lawyer
rechtzeitig on time
Regen *m* rain
Regenbogen *m* rainbow
Regenmantel *m* raincoat
Regierung *f* government
regnen rain; **es regnet** it's
  raining
reich rich
reichen: das reicht that's
  enough
reif ripe
Reifen *m* tyre
Reifenpanne *f* puncture

GERMAN-ENGLISH

reinigen clean
Reinigung f laundry
Reinigungscreme f cleansing cream
Reis m rice
Reise f journey
Reisebüro n travel agent's
Reiseführer m guide; guidebook
reisen travel
Reiseproviant m food for the journey
Reisescheck m traveller's cheque
Reißverschluß m zip
Reitsport m horse riding
Rentner m, **Rentnerin** f old-age pensioner
reparieren mend, repair
reservieren reserve
Reservierung f reservation
Rezept n recipe; prescription
Rezeption f reception
Rheuma n rheumatism
richtig right; correct
Richtung f direction
riechen smell
Riegel m bolt
Rindfleisch n beef
Rippe f rib
Rock m skirt; rock music
roh raw
Rohr n pipe
Rollstuhl m wheelchair
Roman m novel
Röntgenaufnahme f X-ray
rosa pink
Rosenkohl m Brussels sprouts
rot red
Röteln pl German measles
rothaarig red-headed

Rotwein m red wine
Rücken m back
Rückfahrkarte f return ticket
Rücklichter npl rear lights
Rücksitz m back seat
Rückspiegel m rearview mirror
Rückwärtsgang m reverse gear
Ruderboot n rowing boat
rufen call; shout
Ruhe f rest; **Ruhe!** quiet!
ruhig quiet
Rühreier npl scrambled eggs
Ruinen fpl ruins
rund round

Sache f thing
Saft m juice
sagen say
sagenhaft terrific
Sahne f cream
Salat m salad; lettuce
Salatsoße f salad dressing
Salbe f ointment
Salon m lounge
Salz n salt
salzig salty
Sammlung f collection
Samstag m Saturday
Sandalen fpl sandals
Satz m sentence; rate
sauber clean
sauer sour
Säuglingstragetasche f carry-cot
Schachtel f box; packet

schade: das ist schade it's a pity
Schädel m skull
Schaf n sheep
Schaffner m conductor
Schal m scarf
Schallplatte f record
Schalter m switch
Schaltknüppel m gear lever
schämen: sich schämen be ashamed
scharf sharp; hot
Schatten m shade
Schauer m shower
Scheck m cheque
Scheckheft n cheque book
Scheckkarte f cheque card
Scheibe f slice
Scheibenwischer m windscreen wiper
scheinen shine; seem
Scheinwerfer mpl headlights
Schenkel m thigh
Schere f scissors
scheu shy
Schiff n ship; boat
Schild n sign
Schinken m ham
Schirm m umbrella
Schlafanzug m pyjamas
schlafen sleep; **sie schläft** she's asleep
Schlaflosigkeit f insomnia
Schlafsack m sleeping bag
Schlaftablette f sleeping pill
Schlafwagen m sleeper
Schlafzimmer n bedroom
schlagen hit
Schlagsahne f whipped cream
Schlange f snake; queue; **Schlange stehen** queue
schlank slim

Schlauch m inner tube
schlecht bad(ly); **mir ist schlecht** I feel sick
schlechter worse
schlechteste worst
schleudern skid
schließen close
Schließfach n luggage locker
Schloß n castle; lock
Schluckauf m hiccups
Schlüssel m key
Schmerz m pain
schmerzen hurt
schmerzhaft painful
Schmerzmittel n painkiller
Schmetterling m butterfly
Schmuck m jewellery
schmutzig dirty
schnarchen snore
Schnecke f snail
Schnee m snow
schneiden cut
schneien snow
schnell fast
Schnurrbart m moustache
Schnürsenkel mpl shoe laces
Schock m shock
Schokolade f chocolate
schon already
schön beautiful; fine
schottisch Scottish
Schottland n Scotland
Schrank m cupboard
Schraube f screw
Schraubenschlüssel m spanner; wrench
Schraubenzieher m screwdriver
schreiben write
Schreibmaschine f typewriter
Schreibpapier n writing paper

Schreibwarenladen *m* stationer's
schreien scream
Schuhcreme *f* shoe polish
Schuhe *mpl* shoes
Schuhmacher *m* shoe repairer
schuld: ich bin/er ist schuld it's my/his fault
Schule *f* school
Schulter *f* shoulder
Schüssel *f* bowl
schützen protect
schwach weak
Schwager *m* brother-in-law
Schwägerin *f* sister-in-law
schwanger pregnant
Schwanz *m* tail
schwarz black
schwarz-weiß black and white
Schwein *n* pig
Schweinefleisch *n* pork
Schweiz *f* Switzerland
Schweizer Swiss
schwer heavy; difficult
Schwester *f* sister
Schwiegersohn *m* son-in-law
Schwiegertochter *f* daughter-in-law
Schwiegervater *m* father-in-law
schwierig difficult
Schwimmbad *n* swimming pool
Schwimmen *n* swimming
schwimmen swim; **schwimmen gehen** go swimming
schwitzen sweat
See *m* lake
See *f* sea
seekrank seasick

Segelboot *n* sailing boat
Segeln *n* sailing
sehen see
sehr very
Seide *f* silk
Seife *f* soap
Seil *n* rope
sein be
sein, seine his
seit since
Seite *f* side; page
Sekunde *f* second
selbe same
selbst: er/sie selbst he himself/she herself; **selbst Männer/wenn** even men/if
Selbstbedienung *f* self-service
selbstverständlich of course
selten rare
seltsam strange
senden send
Senf *m* mustard
sensibel sensitive
Sessellift *m* chairlift
setzen: sich setzen sit down
sexistisch sexist
sicher sure; safe
Sicherheitsgurt *m* seat belt
Sicherheitsnadel *f* safety pin
Sicherung *f* fuse
sie she; her; they; them
Sie you
Silber *n* silver
singen sing
sinken sink
Sitz *m* seat
skandalös shocking
skifahren ski
Skifahren *n* skiing
Skipiste *f* ski slope
Skistiefel *mpl* ski boots
so so; this way; **ach so!** I

see
Socken *fpl* socks
sofort immediately
Sohle *f* sole
Sohn *m* son
Sommer *m* summer
Sommerferien *pl* summer
holidays
sondern but
Sonnabend *m* Saturday
Sonne *f* sun
sonnenbaden sunbathe
Sonnenbrand *f* sunburn
Sonnenbrille *f* sunglasses
Sonnenöl *n* suntan lotion/oil
Sonnenschein *m* sunshine
Sonnenstich *m* sunstroke
Sonnenuntergang *m* sunset
sonnig sunny
Sonntag *m* Sunday
sonst otherwise
Sorge *f* worry; **sich Sorgen
machen (um)** worry (about)
Soße *f* sauce
Souterrain *n* basement
sowieso anyway
Spanien *n* Spain
Spargel *m* asparagus
Sparkasse *f* savings bank
spät late; **wie spät ist es?**
what time is it?
Spaten *m* spade
spazieren gehen go for a
walk
Spaziergang *m* walk
Speck *m* bacon
Speiche *f* spoke
Speisekarte *f* menu
Speisewagen *m* dining car
Speisezimmer *n* dining room
Spezialität *f* speciality
Spiegel *m* mirror
Spiel *n* game; match

spielen play
Spielzeug *n* toy
Spinat *m* spinach
Spinne *f* spider
Spirale *f* spiral; IUD
Spitzer *m* pencil sharpener
Spitzname *m* nickname
Sporttauchen *n* skin-diving
Sportwagen *m* sports car;
pushchair
Sprache *f* language
Sprachenschule *f* language
school
Sprachführer *m* phrase book
sprechen speak; talk
Sprechstunde *f* surgery
springen jump
Spritze *f* injection
Spüle *f* sink
Spülmittel *n* washing-up
liquid
Staatsangehörigkeit *f*
nationality
Stadt *f* town; city
Stadtmitte *f* city centre
Stadtplan *m* map
Standlicht *n* sidelights
stark strong
Stau *m* traffic jam
Staubsauger *m* vacuum
cleaner
stechen sting
Stechmücke *f* mosquito
Steckdose *f* socket
Stecker *m* plug
stehen stand; **blau steht
Ihnen** blue suits you
stehlen steal
steil steep
Stein *m* stone
Stelle *f* place
sterben die
Stern *m* star

113

Stich *m* bite
Stiefel *m* boot
Stiefmutter *f* stepmother
Stiefvater *m* stepfather
Stift *m* pen
still quiet
Stille *f* silence
stillen breastfeed
Stimme *f* voice
Stimmung *f* mood
Stirn *f* forehead
Stock *m*: **erster Stock** first floor
Stoff *m* material
stolz proud
Stöpsel *m* plug
stören disturb; **stört es Sie, wenn ich ...?** do you mind if I ...?; **bitte nicht stören** please do not disturb
Stoßdämpfer *m* shockabsorber
Stoßstange *f* bumper
Strafe *f* penalty; fine
Strand *m* beach
Straße *f* street; road
Straßenbahn *f* tram
Straßenbauarbeiten *fpl* roadworks
Straßenverkehrsordnung *f* highway code
Strecke *f* route
streichen paint; cancel
Streichholz *n* match
stricken knit
Stromausfall *m* power cut
Strümpfe *mpl* stockings
Strumpfhose *f* tights
Stück *n* piece; play
Stuhl *m* chair
Stunde *f* hour; lesson
Sturm *m* storm
suchen look for

Sucher *m* viewfinder
Süden *m* south
südlich von south of
Supermarkt *m* supermarket
Suppe *f* soup
süß sweet

Tabak *m* tobacco
Tablett *n* tray
Tablette *f* tablet
Tacho *m* speedometer
Tafelwein *m* house wine
Tag *m* day; **guten Tag** hello
Tagebuch *n* diary
Tageskarte *f* set menu
täglich daily
Taille *f* waist
Tal *n* valley
Tankstelle *f* petrol station
Tante *f* aunt
tanzen dance
Tasche *f* pocket; bag
Taschendieb *m* pickpocket
Taschenlampe *f* torch
Taschenmesser *n* penknife
Taschenrechner *m* calculator
Taschentuch *n* handkerchief
Tasse *f* cup
taub deaf
tauchen dive
tauschen exchange
Tee *m* tea
Teekanne *f* teapot
Teich *m* pond
teilen share
Telefonbuch *n* phone book
Telefonnummer *f* phone number

Telefonzelle *f* phone box
Teller *m* plate
Teppich *m* carpet
Tesafilm (R) *m* sellotape (R)
teuer expensive
Thermosflasche *f* thermos
  flask
Thunfisch *m* tuna fish
tief deep; low
Tiefkühlkost *f* frozen food
Tier *n* animal
Tierarzt *m* vet
Tiergarten *m* zoo
Tisch *m* table
Tischdecke *f* tablecloth
Tischtennis *n* table tennis
Tochter *f* daughter
Tod *m* death
Toilette *f* toilet
Toilettenpapier *n* toilet
  paper
Tomate *f* tomato
Torte *f* tart
tot dead
töten kill
tragen carry
Trainingsanzug *m* tracksuit
trampen hitchhike
Trampen *n* hitchhiking
Trauben *fpl* grapes
Traum *m* dream
traurig sad
treffen meet
Treffen *n* meeting
Treppe *f* stairs
Trichter *m* funnel
trinken drink
Trinkgeld *n* tip
Trinkwasser *n* drinking
  water
trocken dry
trocknen dry
Tropfen *m* drop

Truthahn *m* turkey
tun do; put
Tür *f* door
Turm *m* tower
Turnschuhe *mpl* trainers

U-Bahn *f* underground
über over; above
überall everywhere
übergeben hand over; **sich**
  übergeben be sick
Übergewicht *n* overweight;
  excess baggage
überholen overtake
übermorgen the day after
  tomorrow
überqueren cross
überraschend surprising
Überraschung *f* surprise
übersetzen translate
übertreiben exaggerate
üblich usual
Ufer *n* shore
Uhr *f* clock; **um 5 Uhr**
  morgens at 5 a.m.; **um 23**
  Uhr/11 Uhr abends at 11
  p.m.
um around; **um drei Uhr** at
  3 o'clock
Umleitung *f* diversion
Umschlag *m* envelope
umsteigen change trains/
  buses *etc*
umstoßen knock over
umziehen: sich umziehen
  change
unabhängig independent
unangenehm unpleasant

und and
Unfall *m* accident
ungefähr approximately
unglaublich incredible
unhöflich rude
Universität *f* university
unmöglich impossible
uns us
unschuldig innocent
unser, uns(e)re our
Unsinn *m* nonsense
unten downstairs;
  underneath; **unten an/in** at
  the bottom of; **dort unten**
  down there
unter below, under;
  underneath; among
Unterkunft *f* accommodation
untersagt prohibited
unterschreiben sign
Unterschrift *f* signature
Untertasse *f* saucer
Unterwäsche *f* underwear
uralt ancient
Urlaub *m* holiday

Vater *m* father
Vati *m* dad
vegetarisch vegetarian
Ventil *n* valve
Ventilator *m* fan
Verabredung *f* appointment
verantwortlich responsible
Verband *m* bandage;
  association
verbergen hide
verbessern improve
Verbindung *f* connection

verboten forbidden;
  prohibited
Verbrennung *f* burn
Vereinigte Staaten *fpl* United
  States
Vergaser *m* carburettor
vergessen forget
Vergewaltigung *f* rape
Vergrößerung *f* enlargement
verheiratet married
Verhütungsmittel *n*
  contraceptive
Verkauf *m* sale
verkaufen sell; **zu**
  verkaufen for sale
Verkehr *m* traffic
Verkehrspolizist *m* traffic
  warden
Verkehrszeichen *n* roadsign
verlangen ask for
Verlängerungsschnur *f*
  extension lead
verletzt injured
verlieren lose
verlobt engaged
Verlobte *m/f* fiancé; fiancée
vermieten: zu vermieten for
  hire; to let
vermissen miss
vernünftig sensible
verpassen miss
verriegeln bolt
verrückt mad
verschieden different
verschlucken swallow
Verschluß *m* shutter
verschmutzt polluted
verschwinden disappear;
  verschwinden Sie! go
  away!
Versicherung *f* insurance
verspätet late, delayed
Verspätung *f* delay

versprechen promise
verstauchen sprain
verstehen understand
verstopft blocked; constipated
versuchen try
Verteiler m distributor
Vertreter m agent
Verzeihung! sorry!
Verzögerung f delay
Vetter m cousin
viel much, a lot (of)
viele many
vielleicht maybe
Viertel n quarter; district
violett purple
Visitenkarte f card
Visum n visa
Vitamine npl vitamins
Vogel m bird
voll full; crowded
Vollkornbrot n wholemeal bread
Vollmilchschokolade f milk chocolate
Vollpension f full board
von of; by; **von Nürnberg nach Hannover** from Nuremberg to Hanover
vor before; in front of; **vor drei Tagen** three days ago
voraus: im voraus in advance
vorbei over; **vorbei an ...** past ...
vorbereiten prepare
Vorderseite f front
Vorfahr m ancestor
Vorfahrt f right of way
vorgestern the day before yesterday
Vorhang m curtain
Vorname m Christian name, first name

vorsichtig careful
Vorspeise f starter
Vorstadt f suburbs
vorstellen introduce
Vorwahl f dialling code
vorziehen prefer

wach awake
Wagen m car; coach; carriage
wagen dare
Wagenheber m jack
wählen choose; dial
wahr true
während during; while
wahrscheinlich probably
Wald m forest
walisisch Welsh
Wand f wall
wann when
warm warm
Wärme f heat
Wärmflasche f hot-water bottle
warten wait
Wartesaal m waiting room
warum? why?
was? what?
Waschbecken n washbasin
Wäsche f washing; laundry
Wäscheklammer f clothes peg
waschen wash; **sich waschen** wash
Wäscherei f laundry
Waschmaschine f washing mashine

Waschpulver *n* washing powder
Waschsalon *m* launderette
Wasser *n* water
Wasserfall *m* waterfall
Wasserhahn *m* tap
Wasserkessel *m* kettle
Wasserski *n* waterskiing
Watte *f* cotton wool
wechselhaft changeable
Wechselkurs *m* exchange rate
wechseln change
Wechselstube *f* bureau de change
wecken wake up
Wecker *m* alarm clock
weder ... noch ... neither ... nor ...
Weg *m* path
weggehen go away
wegnehmen take away
wegwerfen throw away
weh tun hurt
weich soft
Weihnachten Christmas
weil because
Wein *m* wine
Weinberg *m* vineyard
Weinbrand *m* brandy
weinen cry
Weinhandlung *f* off-licence
Weinkarte *f* wine list
weiß white
Weißbrot *n* white bread
Weißwein *m* white wine
weit far; **weit entfernt** far away
weiter further
welche? which?
Welle *f* wave
Welt *f* world
wenden turn; **sich wenden**

an contact
wenig little; **wenig Touristen** few tourists
weniger less
wenn when
wer? who?
Werbung *f* advertising
werden become; will
werfen throw
Werktag *m* weekday
Werkzeug *n* tool
Wespe *f* wasp
Westen *f* west
westlich von west of
Wetter *n* weather
Wetterbericht *m* weather forecast
wichtig important
widerlich disgusting
widerwärtig obnoxious
wie like; **so schön wie** as beautiful as
wie? how?; wie viele? how many?
wiederholen repeat
wieviel? how much?
Wild *n* game
Wildleder *n* suede
willkommen! welcome!
Wimperntusche *f* mascara
Wind *m* wind
Windbeutel *m* cream puff
Windel *f* nappy
Windeleinlagen *fpl* nappy-liners
Windschutzscheibe *f* windscreen
wir we
wirklich really
wissen know; **ich weiß nicht** I don't know
Witwe *f* widow
Witwer *m* widower

Witz *m* joke
wo? where?
woanders elsewhere
Woche *f* week
Wochenende *n* weekend
woher? where from?
wohin? where to?
wohnen live; stay
Wohnung *f* flat
Wohnwagen *m* caravan
Wohnzimmer *n* living room
Wolke *f* cloud
Wolle *f* wool
wollen want
Wort *n* word
Wörterbuch *n* dictionary
Wunde *f* wound
wunderbar wonderful
Wurst *f* sausage
Würstchen *n* frankfurter
wütend furious

zahlen pay
Zahn *m* tooth
Zahnarzt *m* dentist
Zahnbürste *f* toothbrush
Zahnpasta *f* toothpaste
Zahnschmerzen *mpl*
　toothache
Zange *f* pliers
Zaun *m* fence
z.B. eg
Zehe *f* toe
zeigen show
Zeit *f* time
Zeitung *f* newspaper
Zelt *n* tent
Zentralheizung *f* central
　heating

Zentrum *n* centre
zerbrechen break
Zeuge *m* witness
Ziege *f* goat
ziehen pull
ziemlich rather
Zigarette *f* cigarette
Zigarre *f* cigar
Zimmer *n* room
Zimmermädchen *n*
　chambermaid
Zimmernachweis *m*
　accommodation service
Zitrone *f* lemon
Zitronentee *m* lemon tea
Zoll *m* customs
zollfrei duty-free
zu to; too; shut
Zucker *m* sugar
Zufall *m*: **durch Zufall** by
　chance
zufrieden pleased
Zug *m* train; draught
zuhören listen
Zukunft *f* future
zum to the; **zum Ochsen**
　The Ox (*pub etc name*)
zunächst first(ly)
Zündkerze *f* spark plug
Zündung *f* ignition
Zunge *f* tongue
zur to the
zurück back
zurückgeben give back
zurückkehren return
zurückkommen come back
zusammen together
Zusammenstoß *m* crash
Zuschauer *m* spectator
Zuschlag *m* supplement
Zustand *m* state
Zwiebel *f* onion
zwischen between

GRAMMAR

German has three *GENDERS*, masculine (*m*), feminine (*f*) and neuter (*n*). For masculine nouns the definite article (the) is **der** and the indefinite article (a, an) is **ein**:

der Mann	the man
der Tisch	the table
ein Mann	a man
ein Tisch	a table

For feminine nouns the word for 'the' is **die** and the word for 'a' is **eine**:

die Frau	the woman
die Straße	the street
eine Frau	a woman
eine Straße	a street

For neuter nouns the word for 'the' is **das** and the word for 'a' is **ein**:

das Kind	the child
das Tier	the animal
ein Kind	a child
ein Tier	an animal

The plural of the definite article (the) for all three genders is **die**:

die Tische	the tables
die Straßen	the streets
die Tiere	the animals

The forms of the definite and indefinite articles undergo certain changes according to their case (nominative, accusative, genitive or dative):

	m	*f*	*n*	*pl*
nom	der	die	das	die
acc	den	die	das	die
gen	des	der	des	der
dat	dem	der	dem	den
nom	ein	eine	ein	
acc	einen	eine	ein	
gen	eines	einer	eines	
dat	einem	einer	einem	

GRAMMAR

der Briefträger gab der Frau das Geld
the postman (*nom*) gave the woman (=*dat*) the money
(=*acc*)

ich habe eine Woche des Urlaubs in den Bergen verbracht
I spent a week (=*acc*) of the holiday (=*gen*) in the
mountains (=*dat*)

For the formation of the *PLURAL* of nouns only few general
rules can be given. Many nouns form their plural by adding **-e**:

der Tag	**die Tage**	day(s)
der Preis	**die Preise**	price(s)

Others, in particular words of foreign origin, add **-s**:

das Hotel	**die Hotels**	hotel(s)
das Taxi	**die Taxis**	taxi(s)

Some nouns, like those ending in **-chen** or **-sel**, do not change
at all:

das Mädchen	**die Mädchen**	girl(s)
der Wechsel	**die Wechsel**	change(s), draft(s)

Here are some noun endings which follow a regular pattern to
form their plural:

noun ending	*plural*
-e	**-en**
-heit	**-heiten**
-in	**-innen** (*feminine nouns only*)
-keit	**-keiten**
-schaft	**-schaften**
-ung	**-ungen** (*feminine nouns only*)

Some examples:

die Stunde	**die Stunden**	hour(s)
die Studentin	**die Studentinnen**	female student(s)
die Rechnung	**die Rechnungen**	bill(s), invoice(s)

Note that sometimes the vowels **a**, **o** or **u** of a noun change to
'umlauts' (**ä**, **ö** or **ü**) in the plural:

der Floh	**die Flöhe**	flea(s)
die Kuh	**die Kühe**	cow(s)
das Haus	**die Häuser**	house(s)

GRAMMAR

German *ADJECTIVES* have to agree with their noun, which means they change their endings according to the noun's gender (masculine, feminine or neuter) and case (nominative, accusative, genitive or dative); the ending will also depend on whether the noun is used with the definite (**der, die, das**) or indefinite article (**ein, eine, ein**).

The ending for genitive and dative is **-en** throughout:

> **der Preis des/eines guten Weines**
> the price of the/a good wine

> **in dem/einem ruhigen Hotel**
> in the/a quiet hotel

> **in deutschen Gaststätten**
> in German pubs

The nominative and accusative endings for adjectives used with **der, die** or **das** are as follows:

	m	*f*	*n*	*pl*
nom	-e	-e	-e	-en
acc	-en	-e	-e	-en

das ist der gute Wein	that's the good wine (*nom*)
ich kaufte den guten Wein	I bought the good wine (*acc*)
das gesunde Klima	the healthy climate (*nom or acc*)

When used with **ein** or **eine** (or with no article at all) the endings are:

	m	*f*	*n*
nom	-er	-e	-es
acc	-en	-e	-es

das ist ein guter Wein	that's a good wine (*nom*)
ich kaufte einen guten Wein	I bought a good wine (*acc*)
ein gesundes Klima	a healthy climate (*nom or acc*)
guter Wein ist teuer	good wine is expensive
gesundes Klima	(a) healthy climate

The plural ending of adjectives used without an article is always **-e**:

> **gute Weine**   good wines

Note that the case of an article or an adjective is often determined by *PREPOSITIONS*, which may take the accusative or dative.

GRAMMAR

The following prepositions are used with the accusative:

bis	durch	für	gegen	ohne	um
until	through	for	against	without	around, at

The following prepositions are used with the dative:

aus	außer	bei	gegenüber
from	except	at	opposite

mit	nach	von	zu
with	after, to	from	to, at

Some prepositions take either accusative or dative, depending on whether they indicate movement (*acc*) or position (*dat*):

an	auf	hinter	in
on(to), at	on(to)	behind	in(to)

neben	über	unter	vor	zwischen
beside	over	under	before	between

| er setzte sich neben mich | he sat down beside me (=*acc*) |
| er saß neben mir | he was sitting beside me (=*dat*) |

COMPARATIVES are formed by adding **-er** to the adjective:

| schön | beautiful |
| schöner | more beautiful |

SUPERLATIVES are formed with **der/die/das . . . -ste**

| das billigste Hotel | the cheapest hotel |

POSSESSIVE ADJECTIVES have to agree with the gender of the noun they refer to:

	m	*f*	*n*	*pl*
my	mein	meine	mein	meine
your	Ihr	Ihre	Ihr	Ihre
your (*fam*)*	dein	deine	dein	deine
his/its	sein	seine	sein	seine
her/its	ihr	ihre	ihr	ihre
our	unser	unsere	unser	unsere
your	Ihr	Ihre	Ihr	Ihre
your (*fam*)*	euer	eure	euer	eure
their	ihr	ihre	ihr	ihre

* familiar form if using **du** (singular) and **ihr** (plural) for 'you'.

meine Frau	my wife
unser Urlaub	our holiday
Ihre Brieftasche	your wallet

GRAMMAR

PERSONAL PRONOUNS

subject		object		indirect object	
ich	I	mich	me	mir	to me
Sie	you	Sie	you	Ihnen	to you
du	you	dich	you	dir	to you (*fam*)
er	he/it	ihn	him/it	ihm	to him/it
sie	she/it	sie	her/it	ihr	to her/it
es	it	es	it	ihm	to it
wir	we	uns	us	uns	to us
Sie	you	Sie	you	Ihnen	to you
ihr	you	euch	you	euch	to you (*fam*)
sie	they	sie	them	ihnen	to them

ich habe sie Ihnen gegeben I gave them to you
sie hat es uns gesagt she told us (about it)
ich treffe ihn morgen I'll be meeting him tomorrow

The German for 'it' will not always be **es**; it can also be **er** or **sie**, depending on the gender of the word it replaces:

diese Stadt, sie ist sehr alt this town, it's very old
der Rhein? er ist herrlich the Rhine? it's magnificent

There are two words for *YOU* in German. **du** and its forms **dir**, **dich** are used to friends, relatives or children. **Sie** and **Ihnen** are used for someone you don't know as a friend.

With *REFLEXIVE* verbs like **sich erinnern, sich freuen** use the following pronouns:

ich ... mich	wir ... uns
Sie ... sich	Sie ... sich
du ... dich	ihr ... euch
er/sie/es ... sich	sie ... sich

ich erinnere mich I remember
wir freuen uns we are glad

POSSESSIVE PRONOUNS have to agree with the gender of the object possessed:

	m	*f*	*n*	*pl*
mine	meiner	meine	meins	meine
yours	Ihrer	Ihre	Ihres	Ihre
yours (*fam*)	deiner	deine	deins	deine
his/its	seiner	seine	seins	seine
hers/its	ihrer	ihre	ihres	ihre

GRAMMAR

		m	*f*	*n*	*pl*
ours		unserer	unsere	unseres	unsere
yours		Ihrer	Ihre	Ihres	Ihre
yours (*fam*)		eurer	eure	eures	eure
theirs		ihrer	ihre	ihres	ihre

> **das ist nicht Ihr Glas, es ist meins**
> it's not your glass, it's mine

> **hast du deine Schlüssel? ich habe meine verloren**
> have you got your keys? I've lost mine

Note that possession is often expressed with the verb **gehören** (to belong to):

> **dieser Koffer gehört mir**
> this case is mine

German *VERBS*, in their infinitive form as given in the dictionary sections, all end in **-en** or **-n**. They can either be regular or irregular. Irregular verbs undergo vowel changes in certain tenses (see the list of common irregular verbs).

The *PRESENT TENSE* (I buy, he hikes, we are hiking *etc*) is formed as follows:

		kaufen	wandern
		(to buy)	(to hike)
I	ich	kaufe	wand(e)re
you	Sie	kaufen	wandern
you (*fam*)	du	kaufst	wanderst
he/she/it	er/sie/es	kauft	wandert
we	wir	kaufen	wandern
you	Sie	kaufen	wandern
you (*fam*)	ihr	kauft	wandert
they	sie	kaufen	wandern

Two important verbs, 'to be' and 'to have', are irregular:

		sein	haben
		(to be)	(to have)
I	ich	bin	habe
you	Sie	sind	haben
you (*fam*)	du	bist	hast
he/she/it	er/sie/es	ist	hat
we	wir	sind	haben
you	Sie	sind	haben
you (*fam*)	ihr	seid	habt
they	sie	sind	haben

GRAMMAR

The *PAST* is referred to either by the imperfect or the perfect tense. The *IMPERFECT TENSE* is mainly used in stories, newspaper reports and when relating a sequence of events that took place in the past. It is not normally used in conversational German, except for the past tense of the verbs **sein and haben**. The imperfect endings are:

ich	kaufte	wanderte
Sie	kauften	wanderten
du	kauftest	wandertest
er/sie/es	kauftet	wandertet
wir	kauften	wanderten
Sie	kauften	wanderten
ihr	kauftet	wandertet
sie	kauften	wanderten

The imperfect of the verbs **sein** 'to be' and **haben** 'to have' (I was, you were *etc*; I had, you had *etc*) is formed a follows:

ich	war	hatte
Sie	waren	hatten
du	warst	hattest
er/sie/es	war	hatte
wir	waren	hatten
Sie	waren	hatten
ihr	wart	hattet
sie	waren	hatten

The standard case for conversation when talking about the past is the *PERFECT TENSE*. It is formed by adding the appropriate part of the verb **haben**, or, in some cases, the verb **sein**, to the past participle. The *PAST PARTICIPLE* itself is formed by adding **ge-** and **-t** to the 'stem' of the verb, ie its basic form without the **-en** or **-n** ending:

kaufen (= kauf-en) − ge-kauf-t
wandern (= wander-n) − ge-wander-t

ich	habe	gekauft	ich	bin	gewandert
Sie	haben	gekauft	Sie	sind	gewandert
du	hast	gekauft	du	bist	gewandert
er/sie/es	hat	gekauft	er/sie/es	ist	gewandert
wir	haben	gekauft	wir	sind	gewandert
Sie	haben	gekauft	Sie	sind	gewandert
ihr	habt	gekauft	ihr	seid	gewandert
sie	haben	gekauft	sie	sind	gewandert

The verb **haben** uses **haben** to form the past participle; and **sein** uses **sein**. The past participle of **haben** and **sein** are **gehabt** and **gewesen**:

GRAMMAR

ich	habe	gehabt	ich	bin	gewesen
Sie	haben	gehabt	Sie	sind	gewesen
du	hast	gehabt	du	bist	gewesen
etc			*etc*		

The *FUTURE* is formed with **werden** and the infinitive of the verb:

ich	werde	kaufen	ich	werde	wandern
Sie	werden	kaufen	Sie	werden	wandern
du	wirst	kaufen	du	wirst	wandern
er/sie/es	wird	kaufen	er/sie/es	wird	wandern
wir	werden	kaufen	wir	werden	wandern
Sie	werden	kaufen	Sie	werden	wandern
ihr	werdet	kaufen	ihr	werdet	wandern
sie	werden	kaufen	sie	werden	wandern

Some common *IRREGULAR VERBS*:

The forms given are the infinitive (to go), the third persons singular present (he/she goes) and imperfect (he/she went) and the past participle (gone). Verbs marked '+' form their perfect tense with **sein**, all others with **haben**.

bleiben +(*stay*)	bleibt	blieb	geblieben
bringen (*bring*)	bringt	brachte	gebracht
dürfen (*be allowed to*)	darf	durfte	gedurft
essen (*eat*)	ißt	aß	gegessen
fahren + (*drive, go*)	fährt	fuhr	gefahren
finden (*find*)	findet	fand	gefunden
geben (*give*)	gibt	gab	gegeben
gehen + (*go*)	geht	ging	gegangen
haben (*have*)	hat	hatte	gehabt
kennen (*know*)	kennt	kannte	gekannt
kommen +(*come*)	kommt	kam	gekommen
können (*be able to*)	kann	konnte	gekonnt
lassen (*let, allow*)	läßt	ließ	gelassen
lesen (*read*)	liest	las	gelesen
liegen (*lie*)	liegt	lag	gelegen
müssen (*have to*)	muß	mußte	gemußt
nehmen (*take*)	nimmt	nahm	genommen
schreiben (*write*)	schreibt	schrieb	geschrieben
sehen (*see*)	sieht	sah	gesehen
sein + (*be*)	ist	war	gewesen
werden + (*become*)	wird	wurde	geworden
wissen (*know*)	weiß	wußte	gewußt
wollen (*want to*)	will	wollte	gewollt

CONVERSION TABLES

metres
  1 metre = 39.37 inches or 1.09 yards

kilometres
  1 kilometre = 0.62 or approximately ⅝ mile

to convert kilometres to miles: divide by 8 and multiply by 5

kilometres:	2	3	4	5	10	100
miles:	1.25	1.9	2.5	3.1	6.25	62.5

miles
to convert miles to kilometres: divide by 5 and multiply by 8

miles:	1	3	5	10	20	100
kilometres:	1.6	4.8	8	16	32	160

kilos
  1 kilo = 2.2 or approximately 1⅕ pounds

to convert kilos to pounds: divide by 5 and multiply by 11

kilos:	4	5	10	20	30	40
pounds:	8.8	11	22	44	66	88

pounds
  1 pound = 0.45 or approximately 5/11 kilo

litres
  1 litre = approximately 1¾ pints or 0.22 gallons

Celsius
to convert to Fahrenheit: divide by 5, multiply by 9, add 32

Celsius:	10	15	20	25	28	30	34
Fahrenheit:	50	59	68	77	82	86	93

Fahrenheit
to convert Fahrenheit to Celsius: subtract 32, multiply by 5, divide by 9